TABLE OF CONTENTS

For Kathy

Acknowledgments

Thanks to Kathy Eimers Chandler for editing way beyond the norm and support in so many other ways.

To Steve Hardison for the coaching; Darby Checketts for the leverage; Bernadine Mooney for the strength; Fred Knipe for the music and biggest laughs; Terry Hill for the blood oath and the pursuit of Moby-Dick; Sam Beckford for being the small business millionaire; Ron and Mary Hulnick for the spirit; Kevin McCarthy for my MOM; Ed and Jeanne Eimers for the shelter from the storm; Jessica, Stephanie, Mar, and Bobby for the happiness; David Chandler for Thanksgiving; Tom and Danna Fisher for Christmas; John Hersey for the contagious leadership; Jack Calhoun, Jr., for the humor and wisdom; Vic Clough for the storyboard; Michael Bassoff for the story of giving; Sherry Phelan for the great mandalas; Cindy Lou Golin for the light; Ken Wilber for the theory of everything; Rhett Nichols for the care of Grizzly Bear; Lee Dixon for creative mediation; Iyanla Vanzant for the show; Carolyn Freyer-Jones for the brilliant enrollment; Mark Ragel for the commitment to excellence; Dan and Rebecca Bish for the recruiting; Peter and Phil Calihan for the opportunity to teach; Bob Reed for the portal to the world; Jim Manton for living large; Gil Greer for the loss of emotion; Duane Black for allowing success; and Phil Booker for the power of simplicity.

Thanks to Ron Fry and Michael Pye at Career Press for many years of putting books all over the planet.

Thanks to Angus Ross for the brilliant photography.

Thanks to the students of Soul-Centered Leadership at the University of Santa Monica for the best teaching experience of a lifetime.

"And those who were seen dancing were thought to be insane by those who could not hear the music."

—Friedrich Wilhelm Nietzsche

Chapter 1

Where Did You Learn Your Story?

"Every child is born an artist.
The trick is to remain an artist."

—Picasso

There is a place of purity inside every human being that is visited quite often in childhood, but gets talked into oblivion by well-meaning adults who want the young human to grow up and fit in.

Imagine you were that child. And these well-meaning adults wanted you to get busy creating your life. Was it really your life they wanted to shape, or your story? Maybe they wanted to be able to tell *the story of you* to their friends and family, and so you better get busy getting your story going! Only an important story about *who you are* will do. (Not that we can blame the story-pushers. They pushed you into this story-telling because they thought you needed it, as equipment, for your survival.)

Little did they know that this story (the story of you) would get in the way of everything you ever wanted. I mean that. Everything.

And so who am I to be telling you this about *your* cherished life story? (1) That you just made it up!, and (2) that it gets in the way?

Let's just say I'm Charlie Lau.

I'm not literally Charlie Lau, because he died in 1994, but Charlie's is the story I now want to tell about myself, and that's my point. We are first the stories we tell, and then we become the story others tell about us.

Baseball's Charlie Lau was a hitting coach who couldn't hit (just as I was a "life coach" who didn't know how to live).

Charlie Lau became the most respected batting coach of his time, although for a long time, he really, truly could not hit. He was a lifetime .180 hitter until 1962. That is when he radically changed his batting style to win a job with the Baltimore Orioles. In desperation, Charlie adopted a contact hitter's stance right out of the 19th century: feet wide apart, bat held almost parallel to the ground. Boy did Charlie look weird! But now he could hit. Finally, he could hit. Because once he took on that old stance, he came alive. He had two hits in an inning he entered as a pinch hitter on June 23, 1962, and doubled four times in one game on July 13 that same year, tying a major league record. His average jumped to .294. He had learned to hit, and soon he was ready to teach what he learned.

His book *How to Hit .300* supplanted Ted Williams's *The Science of Hitting* as the "Bible of Batting." He later taught George Brett to hit nearly .400 many times over. The word was that he was now the best hitting coach ever.

Charlie Lau was obviously not a natural. The baseball movie *The Natural* would never have been inspired by Charlie Lau. But he learned from his struggles. He learned much more about hitting than the so-called "natural hitters" who didn't have to struggle. Maybe it's in the pain and struggle that we humans grow the most. And maybe that's why the best coaches are coaches who have failed a lot. Almost all the best coaches in sports are people you never heard of as players.

In his book, *The Myth of Mental Illness* (Harper & Row, 1974), the great psychiatrist Dr. Thomas Szasz once said, "Every act of conscious learning requires the willingness to suffer an injury to one's self-esteem. That is why young children, before they are aware of their own self-importance, learn so easily; and why older persons, especially if vain or important, cannot learn at all."

Grown-up people are almost always vain and important. Don't you notice that? They don't want to admit they don't know anything. Their story depends on their having already learned everything important. They link their self-esteem to feeling complete—as though a nicely finished piece of work.

Take the very important story of *you,* for example. The story of you first got told to you by your parents or guardians and then, internally, got told again by *you* to yourself. Again and again.

But who your parents thought you were was madeup. It was based on their own fears—fears your parents had that you wouldn't "turn out." (I wonder a lot these days if anyone has *ever* turned out. I still hear people's parents say, even about their kids who are in their 30s, "I think he'll *turn out* okay. I hope so, anyway." What are they really saying, these parents? "I hope he doesn't become a serial killer and go on national TV and embarrass me!" That would put a bad ending on their own story. They are their stories, these parents. They aren't who they are, they are the story of who they are.)

The reality of how disempoweringly untrue your story is usually shows up when you have a big problem. If you, yourself, have a problem right now, big or small, you might want to bring it to mind. I'm going to show you how to solve it quickly. Because I believe that what might be stopping you from solving it is your story.

As I talked to my friend Marianne I found out that she was worrying about a big problem of her own. She was a lawyer who had a major case to work on, and she couldn't find the "will" to tackle all the research and early communication that had to be done. Her story wouldn't let her do it. Her story was that she was a procrastinator. Her story said she wasn't a real, grown-up, dependable lawyer at all, but actually a bit of a fake. That was her internal story about herself that she lived with from day to day.

I was Marianne's "coach," and I was very similar to Charlie Lau in that I had learned a new stance for myself based on my own previous inability to hit. In the game of life, I had been, for years, hitting about .180. But my new batting stance gave me some hitting leverage.

"That procrastinator story of yours isn't true," I said to Marianne.

"Oh, it's true," she said. "It's who I am."

"It's a story."

"Well, I say it's my real identity."

"Do you want to solve your current problem?"

"Yes, that's why we're working together. Do you know how to solve it?"

"Yes, I know how you can solve it."

"How?"

"Overwhelm it."

"What?"

"Overwhelm it."

"What exactly do you mean by that?"

"Take massive action from a wild, high-energy state that dwarfs the problem and overwhelms it. Be inappropriate to the problem."

"You want me to be inappropriate?"

"I do."

"In what way?"

"Do not take the appropriate amount of action. Take action that is absurdly disproportionate to the problem. Embarrass the problem. Knock it out of the universe. Smash it, slaughter it, and atomize it with crushing action. Go crazy on it and beat it to a pulp. That's my advice."

Marianne started laughing. But she also started to get interested.

"I could do that," she said hopefully.

"Of course you could," I said.

"It wouldn't be me, though."

"There you go again."

"What? What am I doing?" she asked.

"You are confusing yourself with your story. You are not your story. Your story is madeup."

"Who am I?"

"In this case? You will be overwhelming. That will be who you are."

"I could do this, couldn't I? Okay, I can do this."

And indeed she did. Marianne cleared the decks. She organized her office for pure action. She came to work early and, instead of trying to figure out how much energy she had to give to this project ... instead of trying to be appropriate ... matching her energy appropriately and exactly to the task at hand, she overwhelmed it. She went crazy on it. Nonstop. Hours and hours of manic overkill. She hated the problem and was using pure energy to demolish it.

She didn't leave it at that, either. She also enlisted others. She did marathon phone calling to get other people's energies involved. She asked for help and got it. She laughed and laughed as she took the problem on. The problem didn't have a chance. The problem tried to speak up. It said, "But, but, but,

but...," and she just roared a loud "SHUT UP and TAKE THIS!" and then gave her problem 100 more whacks.

When I met with Marianne a few weeks later I asked her how the legal hearing went and she said, "I won. Big time. Everyone involved was stunned. The other party virtually gave up. Hell hath no fury, I guess."

"Hell hath no fury? What do you mean by that?"

"Hell hath no fury like that of a woman scorned."

"How do you feel you were scorned?"

"I was scorned by my problem. I was mocked and humiliated by it. I was made to feel less than I was. There was a little girl in me that wasn't being looked after and I was allowing that little girl to believe all kinds of negative things about herself, as if she wasn't a fit for the grown-up world, and she wasn't enough, and she was a procrastinator."

"Those are just stories."

"Right!"

"So what's your new story?"

"Internally?"

"Yes. Start there."

"I don't need or want a story. I want to be able to just get into direct action. Story-less action. Based on the purpose I choose."

"Perfect. Now what about the external story?"

"I'm the toughest-minded and best-prepared attorney in town."

"There you go."

"But is that true?"

"You tell me!"

"It is, but it's not. But how was I able to do it if it wasn't true?"

"You made it true in the moment you took action. And you can make anything true in the moment. Just go to that place of purity and power. Remember that. But you have to get into the moment and out of your story."

When Dr. Thomas Szasz says, as he does in his words quoted earlier, that you have to suffer an injury to your self-esteem to learn something new, he is right! And when he says that's why adults hate learning anything new, he is right about that too, because subconsciously adults know that they will have to injure themselves—or, to put it another way, they'll have to give up their story.

Chapter 2

Chaos Is the Highest Form of Order?

"I accept chaos. I'm not sure whether it accepts me."

—Bob Dylan

I risk injury to my own self-esteem by getting coaching from a wonderful and powerful coach. So I learn something new almost every time. And I give up old stories. I replace them with new ones. The faster the better.

Like the story of chaos that I used to tell about myself. The story said that I created chaos everywhere I went. That I was disorganized. That I needed to change. That there was something wrong with me. That I didn't measure up to organized adults. That I wasn't enough.

It always gets down to that, doesn't it? The story of me is the same story as the story of Marianne. Or the story of you. The story says we're not enough, as is. Who we are is *not enough.* Isn't this the story of you, too? Try it out. Say over and over, "Who I am is not enough," and see if it resonates and feels "true" about you. Then try changing the statement. Start saying, now, "TRUE STORY: Who I am is *more* than enough!" Finish your session by saying, "That's my new story, and my life is about making it true in this present moment."

So my story was chaos.

"What's wrong with chaos?" asked my business consultant, the amazing Mr. Steve Hardison.

I said, "Well, it shouldn't be so. Chaos is bad, isn't it? Have you seen my office?"

Hardison said, "I once went to Japan on business and when I got to the office of a very powerful businessman there I noticed that his office looked as if a hurricane had passed through it, and I couldn't believe how disorganized he was until I asked him for certain information and he snatched a document instantly from a pile of papers near him. It was then that I saw that he was fantastically organized, and he knew exactly where everything was. Most people would have to go to some file somewhere and look for a while. He just instantly produced it for me. The most efficient person I'd ever encountered."

I thought about my own office that way, and it was true. I knew where everything was, and I didn't have to sort through filing systems to find anything. I could grab anything right away. It was right there around me. In swirls, maybe, but instantly accessible. No lag time as I sorted through some well-organized file for it.

Hardison said, "Are you familiar with Chaos Theory?"

"Yes," I said. "Or, at least I read a book about how the chaos of the universe only first appears chaotic."

"Right! Chaos is the highest form of order. It's order in a more sophisticated form than the normal, everyday pedestrian order as we know it."

I immediately wanted to put a sign up in my office that said, "CHAOS is the highest form of ORDER."

"You *can* be more organized," said Hardison. "But don't make the chaos wrong. Befriend it.

Welcome it. Only then can you bring it under better control."

In other words, don't have "disorganized" be a part of my bad story. Just figure out what will serve the actions I want to take. There's no story at all in that.

I started to organize my office and work differently. Rather than look at the "mess," heave a big sigh, and wonder why I am so dysfunctional, I now admire what's around me. I look upon it with wonder and happiness. Look at the swirling abundance here. Look at the opportunity for connecting with people, spinning all around me. Let me guide some of this swirling. Just as a glassblower guides the hot liquid as it spins, let me shape this chaos to suit my mission. The old story evaporated.

Chapter 3

Are You a Story Told by an Idiot?

"Stories are equipment for living."

—Kenneth Burke

Now for a story I tell in which I'm the hero. Just let me do this. My other books are interspersed with stories of my being sometimes pathetic, often the loser, a coward, an addict, a bankrupt failure, and so on. So it should be okay to have one in which I am uncommonly strong.

So it's right after 9/11 and, if you don't remember, it was a horrible time economically for many people. Planes weren't flying, and business was in a slowed-down stall.

It was especially troublesome for people in the line of work who give seminars for a living, because we travel to conventions and retreats, and most of those events had all been canceled!

Well, it was during a time when I simply couldn't afford to have cash flow slow-down, so I used my old, faithful thinking tool: "WHAT'S GOOD ABOUT THIS?" It is really an amazing tool to use, and almost no one I know of thinks to use it—even after I teach it to them. (Even I don't use it as often as I could.) But it is a great story-changer! Usually I use it in a crisis when I *know* I need to rise above circumstances. Here's how the thinking tool works: After the shock of something gone horribly wrong has worn off a bit, you simply ask, "Okay, *what's good* about this?" Then ask, "Where's the gift in this?"

So I started asking myself that question about conventions and seminars being canceled all over America. Soon I started calling all kinds of organizations that had to cancel their big sales meetings, retreats, and conventions. I said, basically, "I know you are unable to have your national sales meeting right now like you wanted to. And I also know that, with the impact of 9/11, morale for your people can't be too great. So this is exactly the time when they could use a shot in the arm. So I want to be your solution. I want to bring your convention to your door and to your people by creating tailor-made CDs for them to drive around listening to, creating an exciting eMotivator/eCoaching program where they'll get coaching and regular motivational messages from me, and also by hooking everyone up to an exciting 50-minute teleconference and sending new books to everyone in your organization every month to get them uplifted and psyched."

Companies became fascinated by my offer, and I wound up doing more business than I had ever done before. I was using the business downturn aftermath of 9/11 as a kite uses the wind.

But here's the funny part.

In the middle of all this new business I was signing up, I happened to join a group of professional public speakers for lunch one day to talk shop and share anecdotes about the speaking business. They were complaining about how 9/11 had harmed their business. Here's the humor and irony in this: These are the same public speakers who, when given a chance to speak, will be powerful and eloquent and shout to their audiences about the wisdom of *rising above* circumstances! They give whole motivational talks on "Turning Stumbling Blocks into Stepping Stones!" Yet when they themselves encountered 9/11, they froze. They choked. Then they whined and moaned. For years after! Not understanding how pathetic they were.

They didn't understand because their stories were true for them. They needed their stories to explain their weak performances. Stories are indeed equipment for living, and for explaining a life in which external events have seemed overwhelming.

Recently I took on a coaching client who is also a motivational speaker, author, and seminar leader of some repute. I will call him "Mack," for my fun and his anonymity. As I first began meeting with Mack to coach him on expanding his business, he told me the story of his income in the past few years and brought up the "fact" that 9/11 had harmed him financially, as it harmed everyone else in "this business."

"It didn't harm me," I said. "And I'm in this business. Just as you are. In fact, 9/11 helped me a great deal."

"Well, I don't know what you're talking about because 9/11 knocked the wind out of me. I had a bad year because of it. A bad two years, really."

"That's your story, I guess," I said. "But it's not the truth."

"It's not the truth? Hey! Talk to anyone in the speaking industry."

"It's their story, too. I know."

"Are you saying 9/11 didn't harm my business?"

"That's what I'm saying."

"Well, 9/11 happened. And my business went down the tube. So what else could have done that?"

"You. You and how you responded to 9/11."

"How is that?"

"You created a defeated, inadequate response to 9/11."

"Really?"

"Really. And until you can see that, we aren't going to get very far with this coaching."

Mack said nothing. I could tell he was trying to decide if I was right. Finally I could see that he may have become open to revising his story about his career after 9/11.

Mack said, "Okay. So maybe that's true. Maybe it was my weak response to 9/11 that hurt my business. So what needs to change in me?"

"All that needs to change is the story. The *story of you* now says that 9/11 came along, and 9/11 had power and you had no power, so you lost money. You made that story up, just as you might have made up a story about a dragon and a knight and a maiden for one of your kids one night. It's totally made up. My response to 9/11 got me business because I made up a more useful story for myself."

"What did you make up?"

"I made up that 9/11 was a terrific opportunity for me to help clients who had the wind knocked out of *them* and were wanting something to revive them. I made up that, because so much training was canceled, it created an even greater need for training than before. I made up a story that said 9/11 opened the door to huge opportunities with organizations that were demoralized by canceling company meetings. And by using that story instead of yours, I thrived after 9/11."

"So, my story wasn't a very good story."

"Not very useful. It was good, in a way. It served that part of you that wanted an excuse. Stories always serve some part of us. We think we need our alibis. But it's up to us to find out if they are serving the weak part or the strong part."

"So my story was weak."

"It portrayed *you* as weak and 9/11 as strong. You were not the knight in your story. So the story of you was kind of depressing, really. Ever go to a movie and come out thinking the movie was depressing? I listen to the story of you and 9/11 and I am feeling depressed just listening to it."

Even though Mack made his living teaching other people to find strength in adversity and to look for the lesson in every problem, he was not learning from his own speeches. It was easier for him to live inside a story about himself that made him one more victim of Osama bin Laden.

Even to this day you will hear motivators such as Mack talk about what 9/11 did to them. Other businesspeople, too! I hear this from them all the time. And when I hear it I think that they are the idiots Shakespeare wrote about. And I don't mean that in a negative way. Because they are not "stupid" idiots, really, as much as unconscious people living in stories that are full of sound and fury (the planes CRASHED into the towers, and I was so ANGRY, but I LOST a lot of business!), in Shakespeare's words, as in a tale told by an idiot:

"Life's but a walking shadow, a poor player
That struts and frets his hour upon the stage
And then is heard no more. It is a tale
Told by an idiot, full of sound and fury,
Signifying nothing."

—Macbeth, V.v.

Mack struts and frets after I talk to him about revising his life story so that he, himself, will have more of an active part in it. Right now, he wants to portray himself as a victim of things that happen to him. He wants to say to me that life has happened to him.

But if I'm to work with him at all, I must return him to the source of his power. I can't have him not see the stories he's telling. Because once he sees the stories and their power to limit him, he can tell new ones. We communicate our value through stories, not through claims or sales pitches, but through stories. Mack couldn't see that. He would make up a story, such as the one about 9/11, and then tell it as if it were the truth.

But, it was just a story.

Stories have huge power to alter the whole world. Look at the story of Jesus and Lazarus. It wasn't really raising Lazarus from the dead that impacted the world in such an unforgettable way (indeed, there are groups of scholars now trying to prove that the story was apocryphal), but rather *the story about it.* It was the story of Lazarus that spread around the world and changed the world.

Notice how we subconsciously know all of this already. Inside, at some, we do grasp the power of stories to create who people think we are. People will bring up the name of someone and ask, "What's the story with that guy?"

Or see if this scenario sounds familiar:

"Did you meet our new division manager?"

"Yeah, I met her yesterday, have you?"

"No, not yet. What's her story, anyway?"

And then will you trust what you hear? Sometimes our stories are so divorced from reality it becomes comic. Ask four children who grew up in the same family to individually recount some major event in the family history. Some traumatic moment that everyone should remember. The amazing result is that you will get four entirely different stories. Four different perceptions based on four separate interpretations that create four stories, not one.

What do these stories signify? External reality? Was our dad really that distant and cold? There's no truth to that, just a strange mix of stories and tales told by idiots. The stories say more about the teller's internal fears and hurts than they do about external behavior. We project these stories out onto the world and make the world reflect the inner feeling.

Stories alter external reality to fit our preexisting beliefs.

But what fun when we see and understand this! Because we get in touch with that shaping power we have, as an artist working a spinning wheel of wet clay does. What shall I make Dad into today? And who would I, myself, like to be?

Chapter 4

Silence the Voice in Your Head

"If you hear a voice within you saying
'I am not a painter,'
then, by all means, paint...
and that voice will be silenced."

—Vincent van Gogh

When I first read that quote by van Gogh, a lot of questions came to my mind. First of all, just what *is* that voice I hear that tells me I am not a painter (substitute: teacher, mother, writer, organizer, golfer, lover, good father, anything)?

If you hear a voice that tells you something negative about yourself, who's that voice? You? But then who's the you that's listening? And who's the you that's the voice? People do experience a voice saying something to them. So they say, "I heard a voice saying 'you are not a painter.'" But I wonder who hears that voice? If I'm the voice, then who's hearing me?

Don't we all hear this voice? A lot of times it may say, "Who are you to charge that kind of money?" Or, "Who are you that people would be interested in what you have to say?" Sometimes the voice says, "That's selfish!" or, "You're never organized; you're never grown-up about these things."

But if I can *hear* the voice, I am not the voice, right? If van Gogh could hear the voice that said he was not a painter, he couldn't have been that voice. If you hear a voice down the hall singing, it is not you that is singing.

I know this might seem to be a circular line of thought right now, but it just may be the most important line of thought I'll ever follow. I want to follow this line of thought to wherever it leads. Because that voice has been the one and only thing holding me back in life—*all my life long holding me back*—if it's not really me, I want to know about it. I always *thought* it was me. I thought it was my conscience, at the very least, speaking to me.

But van Gogh says it's just a voice that you can ignore and even disobey.

This voice always seems to tell you the story of how limited you are. It tells you how unworthy you are. It tells you to be careful and watch out before you promise more than you can deliver.

But then our lives lose something. If we listen to the voice, our lives lose their promise.

I think that this voice may have first come into our heads in childhood from the guardian. (We'll call Mom or Dad "the guardian," because many people had no mom or dad, or either, at various stages of their upbringing. So ... who cares? ... it was whatever adult guardian authority figure who knew best. Guardian knows best. Whoever was playing that godlike part at that moment.)

The guardian told you your first stories, including the most important story: *the story of you.* The guardian cared for you, which is to say worried about you, which is to say feared you wouldn't turn out. So those fears coagulated into a story and it became *the story of you* told by this "voice." It was initially the voice of authority. But soon the voice of authority became internalized, and it became the same voice van Gogh talks about, and my same voice that told me not to write this book because it might be too personally revealing and potentially humiliating. Same voice.

Van Gogh said to just ignore the voice if you want to paint. You can silence the voice by painting.

But couldn't that be dangerous? You can't just go out and do *anything,* can you? Let's see. Let's look back on our lives and see just what it is that we *have* accomplished and what it is that we think we can now do. What do we now really have the power to do?

Let's start here, then: *we do what we believe we can do.*

Isn't that right?

Don't we wake up each day and do what we believe is possible to do? If we didn't think it was possible, why would we waste time doing it? Or even thinking about doing it? If I don't believe it's possible for me to play for the Phoenix Suns, I'm not going to pencil in a try-out on my daily calendar. I'm not even going to think about it. We simply ignore things we don't think are possible.

So Step One in the failure of the human being to achieve his or her potential is that the human being only does what he *believes he can do.*

Failure Step Two is this: we only believe we can do what we've done before.

Is that not true? How else do I really believe I can do something? The surest and most common way is to remember that I have done it before. So I say to myself, "I can do this. I've done this before."

But this grim two-step doesn't leave much room for growth. If I only do what I believe I can do—and I only believe I can do what I've done before—then I'm kind of stuck, aren't I? My only possibilities for today are to do what I've done before. Isn't that why most people keep repeating their habits, day after day after day? They find their wheel. They get on it. And go around. They take their places on their own slow-turning mandalas. The voice will keep them turning. In the same way the voice that called to the galley slaves about when to row.

Aren't most people just doing that? Look at them! Rowing their repetitive lives as the galley slaves in *Ben Hur* do. They go to work and do exactly what they've done before. Even their thoughts are thoughts they have thought before. So it's *Groundhog Day* for every one of them. Just live the same day over and over. And when day is done? The same arguments with the spouse. The same frustrated conversations with the kids. The same sarcastic remarks about the boss. Over and over, world without end, round and round, into the ground.

How did van Gogh break out of this spinning wheel of groundhog life? He painted. He disobeyed the voice and painted. We are glad that he did! He painted for us, and we were given a starry, starry night.

Can we be inspired by him? Or someone else? A mentor, even? A spirit guide or a coach? Oh yes. Inspiration is precisely the way off the wheel. The trick is to find a hero. A human inspiration who comes along and wakes us out of the story of us. Snaps us out of the bad dream, breaks the hypnosis of the story, and says, "YOU CAN DO SOMETHING NEW AND SCARY!"

And before we know what we're doing we're doing it. Before the old, limiting voice can be heard, we're just doing it. Before we can check in to see if this bold action matches up with our story about ourselves, we just *do it.*

We just do it.

Before we give the voice a voice *we've already done it.* Van Gogh's voice may try to speak up, but its dim sound is a long way off and he has another voice at his command now that is saying, "SHUT UP, I'M DOING THIS!" And he paints. And he paints.

People hire personal trainers to physically inspire them to do things they did not believe they could do; they're story-busters who work not with your story, but with your body's energy! Your potential! People hire coaches, consultants, and trainers who see their potential and don't care at all about the story that was previously running the show.

My friend Terry Hill had his own negative van Gogh voice that told him he had wasted his life in advertising when he should have been an artist, or a writer of fiction or poetry, or some more elevated pursuit. And now it was too late. "Too late!" said the voice. "It's too late for you." Then he disobeyed the voice. And he started writing. He created a discipline for himself that would bypass the voice. He would write for a minimum of one hour every day. Sometimes more, sometimes a great deal more, but never less, no matter what.

I remember having dinner with him in California when he had recently been at a wedding party that lasted long into the night, and he said it was not easy that night to steal away and do his hour. His promised hour. But the discipline paid off.

Terry not only finished his first book, but he also wrote a play that won a major playwriting competition and was performed in New England to great reviews. He quickly embarked upon his second book and a number of other writing projects. Soon his actions were rewriting the story of Terry. All those years as an advertising creative director and copywriter maybe weren't such a waste. In fact, maybe all those commercials were really, as he began calling them, "playlets," little 30-second and 60-second plays! In fact, maybe his whole life prior to his retirement was the perfect lead-in to his later years as a writer and artist. Now he had the financial freedom to really do it right. New story: new life.

When I wrote a book called *17 Lies,* I wanted to expose how false these self-limiting voices and beliefs were. The idea for the book happened almost by accident when a person I was consulting with started telling me some "truth" about some deep flaw he had as a person: "I'm not very good at.... I've never been good at...." I was very tired that day and had no energy left to give to positive reinforcement, so I just said to him, "You're lying."

He was startled. I was irritated.

I told him he was lying about all that "not good at" stuff. It's not the truth that he was not good at; instead, because he had no idea whether he was any good at that because he'd basically never done anything like that. I told him not to sit there and waste my time and his money by lying and asking me to believe his lies. Would you go to a doctor and lie about your symptoms?

My client was stunned, but I could tell that I had struck a deep chord. Then he started to smile. Finally he said, "You're right. I'm not telling the truth."

So that exchange got me started with my idea of writing a book about the lies people tell themselves. I looked deeply into my own life and found quite a few! (Oh how embarrassing, but write them down anyway, forget the voice....) I looked at the lives of people I had lived with and worked with and I found even more, and finally I had collected 17.

Underneath each lie and motivating each lie was this one: "I am powerless." Because we are not. Because the story can always also be "I am powerful beyond belief." Just as the lawyer Marianne found out.

And that's the key: to learn to get *beyond belief.* To go to that place inside that exists beyond belief. Because it is *belief* that is stifling the power that wants to express itself. The whole point of calling my client a liar was to get him to go beyond his belief. To get to that storyless place that all creative energy comes from.

Chapter 5

Determining the Height of Your Success

*"Don't ask yourself what the world needs.
Ask yourself
what makes you come alive
and then go do it.
Because what the world needs
is people who have come alive."*

—Harold Thurman Whitman

People can lose games, lose money, lose a sales deal, and lose a spouse to divorce without becoming a *loser.*

Losing at something does not require that we create a "loser" story around the event. Instead, we could compose a story that says, "I am brave, bold, and unafraid of losing. I even laugh at defeat."

We could do that, but we rarely do.

Instead, we almost always draw conclusions about ourselves when things go wrong and spin a tale around those conclusions so that we end up living inside a truly painful story.

Just such an example of this made-up myth occurred in 2004 right after the "March Madness" known as the NCAA college basketball tournament. In the late stages of one of the tournament's most crucial games, Memphis was down by two points to Louisville and no time was left on the clock. But it was not yet over for Memphis, because one of their best shooters, Darius Washington, was going to the free-throw line with three shots. If he made all three, his Memphis team would win. If he only made two, they would go into overtime, with a good chance to win. If he made just one, or none, they would lose.

Washington was a 72-percent free-throw shooter, so the Memphis crowd, although holding their collective breath, was counting on at least two shots being made. That would ensure overtime. Three would be heaven. Three would be victory. Darius Washington stepped up to the line with confidence and made his first shot! The crowd, as they say, went crazy. Now all he needed was one of the next two to guarantee overtime. If he hit them both, Memphis would win. He stepped to the line again, but he missed the next free throw. Oh no. Now the tension was huge. One shot left. If he made it: overtime. If he missed it: defeat. Darius shook his arms, and bounced the ball a few times to get himself centered in the moment. Then he shot the ball with perfect form. The ball went up nicely and softly to the rim of the basket and rolled around and off the rim onto the floor! A missed shot! A shocking defeat for Memphis. It was Louisville 75, Memphis 74.

Darius Washington fell to his knees, grabbed his jersey and pulled it over his face as he sobbed. The announcers were speechless, and the whole world watched the crumpled, anguished figure on the floor, a lonely young man in the middle of the basketball court crying his eyes out while the TV cameras zeroed in to capture the painful sight. The drama of the defeat was now supplanted by the drama of this young man's misery. He lost the game for his team. He lost it.

Amazingly, the sight of such gut-wrenching pain in a single human being touched people everywhere. Memphis fans quickly forgot the defeat as they saw how much pain young Darius was in. After the game, the fans flooded hometown talk radio shows to voice their support for young Washington.

Actor Tyrese Gibson was in Toronto filming the
movie *Four Brothers* when he saw the drama
of the game on TV, the missed shots, and
Darius's hopeless anguish on the floor. The
impact on Tyrese was huge. He related and
connected, and was emotionally moved by
Washington's obvious pain. He knew he had to
do something to communicate with this young
man, so he tracked the athlete down days later
and talked to him by phone.

Tyrese wanted Darius Washington to know that
life would be okay and the downs and ups were
all a part of it, and that he was a fine
basketball player who would recover. "I really
felt for him," Tyrese said as reported in a
wonderful story by Grant Wahl in *Sports Illus-
trated.* Tyrese also said, "That was passion
that made him react that way."

Tyrese Gibson knew about the value of passion.
Growing up in Watts, a notoriously rough area
of Los Angeles, the chiseled and handsome
African-American singer-actor-model didn't
always have his sights on stardom. In fact, at
one time in his young life his biggest dream
was to be a garbage man when he grew up.
But by the age of 14, his singing talent had
been discovered, and soon all plans for a career
in sanitation would be left behind as he pursued

a career in entertainment. Abandoned by his father as a little boy, Tyrese struggled in the mean streets of Watts before his passion for music and acting forged his new journey.

Tyrese finally reached young Darius Washington by phone. He told him he saw the game on TV and felt for him. He talked to Darius for a long time, telling him about his own experiences performing under pressure in front of millions. Finally, he gave Darius something that was precious to him. It wasn't anything tangible. It was just some words—a phrase he uses, a daily mantra for motivating himself: "The depth of your struggle will determine the height of your success."

Today, young Darius Washington is back—a bright, cheerful, energetic star player once again. The past is history. His team might have lost that faraway day, but Darius himself is not a loser. Why? Because that's simply not his story.

Most people think "bad" things happen. And then they have to struggle to get over them. And that it's all too bad. And soon the story that gets spun, as a cocoon, around loss or defeat is the story that it "never should have happened." Or that it was "really too bad" that it happened. Pretty soon the person's story accumulates into, "I've had a lot happen to me. A lot of unfortunate events in my life."

These stories do not serve us. They stifle us. They smother us. They spin silky threads around the storyteller so that the storyteller becomes a mummified cocoon, a story-thick lump without any room to move. Without an opportunity for action or grace, or even a chance for a profound ballet dancer's quantum leap into the air.

It's impressive that Tyrese Gibson could see the mummy's threads starting to wind around young Darius while he folded down to his knees and sobbed in the middle of the hardwood basketball court all alone, no one comforting him, and millions watching on TV. Millions. Tyrese had an accurate intuition that his own daily mantra—"The depth of your struggle will determine the height of your success"—would connect with Darius in a place that knows no story.

Chapter 6

What's the Real Secret of Success?

*"You don't need a weatherman
to know which way the wind blows."*

—Bob Dylan

"The real secret of success is enthusiasm," said the great automaker Walter Chrysler. "Yes, more than enthusiasm, I would say excitement. I like to see people get excited. When they get excited they make a success of their lives."

Most people wait for their excitement to happen. They take a ticket and wait. For something. For someone. They sit staring at their ticket, waiting for some factor outside of themselves to call to them and get them excited. Someday my prince will come. Some good fortune. Some lucky event. My company might give me something exciting to work on.

But excitement doesn't work that way. Excitement is an *inner* phenomenon. It starts inside, not outside. People released from solitary confinement get excited about seeing the sun shine. Or seeing a bird in a tree. People who find a new job get excited just driving to work on their first day. Just driving to work excites them! Their excitement is created by their perspective. Their excitement is based on how they are seeing things. And how they see things depends on the lens they are wearing called the story of them.

A couple months after the hurricane Katrina hit Louisiana, *The Carroll County Times* ran an article about a family of nine evacuees who arrived in Westminster, Maryland, without a home or a future.

A church called the Firm Foundation Worship Center heard about the family's plight and got excited about helping them. Marge DiMaggio, the church's co-pastor, was excited about helping these poor people. "They came here with nothing," she said.

Right away, Marge and other church members took over a house on church property and converted it into something that looked and felt to be a real cozy home. They even brought their own pillows over so the family's first night would be comfortable. They quickly laid new carpet donated by a local building company, hung pretty curtains, found appliances, performed a full makeover to make the old-fashioned white-frame house beautiful for the displaced Brown family.

As if that were not enough charity and generosity, they donated food and clothes as well. All for the Brown family, who had lost it all in the hurricane and floods. The Browns were asked to pay no rent and no utilities for the house.

After staying for two months, the Brown family got up and left their new home. They left during church services one Sunday morning. They left unexpectedly. And they left for good. And when church members eventually went to look in the house the Browns had left behind, they were horrified to find it in shambles.

The Carroll County Times report said, "A lamp was smashed on the floor, the lampshade stomped. The screen door was torn off the hinges and flung onto the back deck. Someone cut a hole in the trampoline that belonged to Joann DiMaggio's children. Curtain rods were ripped from the wall and left bent and dangling from one screw. Clothing, potato chip bags, soda cans, socks and empty bags were strewn throughout the house. A hole was punched in a bathroom wall. In another bathroom, dried toothpaste was smeared on the vanity, a cap-less toothpaste tube on the windowsill above. A big, broken pink plastic car was abandoned on the hill outside the house. In a dirty refrigerator upstairs, someone left a coffee mug with an inch or two layer of coffee sludge in the bottom. Dirty dishes were stacked in the sink or on the counters. But in perhaps the biggest insult, the words "MD Sucks" were emblazoned in black paint on the side of the home. 'When our eyes caught this, we all stood here and froze,' Marge DiMaggio said."

According to 42-year-old Keith Brown, who, with his wife and children, was halfway back to his family's home state of Louisiana, the property was not all that misused. "We cleaned up as much as we could," he said. Further, Brown said, the family was never provided with extra money he said the church should have paid to help them return home. "If I wouldn't have done some under-the-table work ... I would never have the money to come home," Brown said.

So according to Mr. Brown, the church did a lot, but not enough. Not enough to avoid the trashing of the home, and the spray-painted "MD SUCKS!" on the side of the home, which the *Times* ran a photo of.

By now you may have an opinion of this story and the people in it. In fact, your opinion, if it is similar to mine, is not very flattering toward Mr. Brown and his family. But that opinion is not shared by everyone. Because we live in a media age that honors victims more than heroes, this was not the end of the story that ran in the newspaper. No, the paper chose to shape this story so that the house-trashers would not look so bad. So they brought in a psychologist by the name of Harald Graning of Confidential Counseling of Westminster so that this story could tilt toward honoring the graffiti-writers a little more.

Graning said the family that trashed the church's house was acting quite normally and naturally. Almost the same way you and I would act in that circumstance. You and I probably would have spray-painted "MD Sucks!" on the wall of our host's home, according to the logic of the psychologist Graning.

"Suppose that you were living your life," he said, "and all of a sudden God came down and destroyed your house? You'd probably be pissed."

That kind of anger needs an outlet, according to Graning. Because you can't just keep it in.

That's unhealthy. That's inauthentic. So whom do you vent it on? God? Well, you might not have immediate access to God. So who else? Well, how about the people who are helping you? Even though you and I might see these church people as being heroes in this story, Graning, with his advanced psychological training, is ready to correct us.

"When you are forced to accept charity," he said, "it's demeaning."

Graning said that doing good only makes the benefactor feel better, not the person being helped. When the person on the receiving end can't repay the kindness and feels compelled to feel appreciative, he or she can become extremely frustrated. Even angry. Acting out can occur. You just can't help it.

And that's how the newspaper story ends. The church members did things that were demeaning to the Brown family. When the house was trashed and defaced, it was because the evacuees were "acting out" something inside them that had nowhere else to go.

End of story.

Except that it's not. Because the psychologist's twisting of the story to make the act of human kindness "demeaning" and the act of property damage "understandable" was so twisted as to mock itself. The story circulated around the Internet, and many who received it thought it was a parody. A satire. They thought it was some joke article from some humorous Website.

"This can't be real," some people said. "I just can't believe that they would run the story like this and give that psychologist the last word."

But it was real. And they did.

After reading the quote at the beginning of the chapter on excitement by Walter Chrysler—one of my favorite observations of all time—and then rereading Chrysler's life story (the short version) on the Internet (the Chrysler building in New York was built by and for him, the successful founder, against all odds, of Chrysler Motors), it really hit home how important it is for a story to ring true. To be taken in, a story needs the ring of truth. And the shining light of the kind of truth that will set you free. As in the story of

Walter Chrysler. And *not* like the story of the poor, misunderstood home-trashers.

For stories to connect, with real power, they must have their own reality. A deeper truth. I personally believe that the story of Lazarus would not have lived to this day had it not really happened.

Many people who have read the story of the messed-up and defaced house in Maryland took as much power and fury from the false conclusion of the psychologist as they did from the inspired actions of the people who turned a house into a new home. They knew it was a false conclusion that evacuees *had* to behave that way.

Because there are other, stronger stories that came from the Katrina hurricane. One family I know of that relocated to a town near mine here in Arizona used the Katrina hurricane to reinvent their lives entirely. They took people's generosity and charity to be an opportunity to start a whole new blessed, focused life. They took the winds and waters of Katrina to be a storm of good fortune, washing away a life of bitterness and poverty in New Orleans.

That's just a story, too, but it created in the minds of the people an inspired life that served them. Whether a wind is a good wind or a bad wind blowing in has more to do with the story you tell than the weather itself.

Two choices are at play when someone gives you a new home to live in after the wind took yours away. You can respond with anger and bitterness, feeling that the gesture was "not enough." Or you can get excited about it. And you can use that excitement to turn your life around.

Chapter 7

A Dose of Sweet Inspiration

"To keep your marriage brimming,
with love in the loving cup,
whenever you're wrong, admit it;
Whenever you're right, shut up."

—Ogden Nash

A teacher–friend named Morey called yesterday to say, "I have noticed a trend. There seems to be a good number of negative-minded teachers around me who are more about asserting their power and control over children than spreading enthusiasm and love."

I think Morey wanted me to join him in condemning those other teachers. Or at least tell him how to change their ways.

But it occurred to me that whenever someone such as Morey is assessing other people's behavior, even though that behavior is first described as something neutral, such as a "trend," the negative judgment has already been made.

The negative story is already there. Morey's story about this "trend" was upsetting him, although he thought it was the trend itself that was upsetting him.

Trends don't upset us. It's our stories about them that upset us.

The problem is never in what's happening around you. The problem is in the internal emotions it triggers. No outside event or behavior "causes" upset by itself. It has to find a memory in your system to link up with to upset you. It's not what's happening that upsets you; it's your inner story about what's happening.

Morey thinks he has a problem because of the people around him. But what he really has a problem with is what's inside him that gets triggered when he *judges* the people around him. Which is to say, when he makes up some story about them.

Morey's story about the cynical teachers around him is that they are "wrong" to be the way they are and he is "right" to be the way he is. That's his story. The problem with those kinds of stories ("I am right and you are wrong") is that they upset us. So now Morey goes into his own classroom after having talked to the other teachers, carrying some upset inside him that he'll have to fight through to really connect with his students. It won't be easy. As we all know, it isn't easy to connect with another human when we are upset about something. Our whole body cries out to other people, "Just go away!" We don't want to connect as much as we want to process the upset.

"Shut up, kids. Sit down! Can't you hear me? I don't want to talk to you right now. I am too upset at the moment trying to deal with these teachers who don't love and embrace kids the way I do and stay joyful and positive about teaching. Sit down or I'll give you detention!"

And so the cycle of judgment is passed on to the children. The poison gets downloaded. The story that says "I'm right and you are wrong" always has a way of ending badly.

When Gandhi said that you can't change other people, but you can "*be* the change you wish to see" in others, there was great practical wisdom in that remark. Most people think it was just some abstract wisdom. Most people hear or read that remark by Gandhi and think, "Well, that was Gandhi, and he was a saint. He was a martyr who fasted. Me? I have to eat. Personally. And I'm not a saint. So how relevant are those words to me?"

But Gandhi's words are very practical! (He was handing us a tool to use, not a quote to make himself look good.) When you read accounts of teachers who inspired whole student bodies and faculties with their enthusiastic and creative approach to teaching, you'll see they never took a moment to criticize the other teachers. As was Robin Williams's character in *Dead Poets Society,* they were too high on the love of teaching to care *at all* what other teachers were doing. And by their example, others were inspired. Not by their judgment, but by their example. People love to be inspired. In fact they wake up every day secretly, subconsciously yearning to be inspired by someone. They hope someone will come along who will wake them out of their cynical stupor, their depressingly bad dream that keeps asking them, "Is this all there is to life? Is this really as good as it gets?"

Sometimes while watching a movie I will cry when something great happens. When someone overcomes an obstacle and wins big against all odds. Why am I crying? Does it make any sense? But maybe I'm crying tears of joy and sorrow simultaneously. Tears of joy because I am inspired. (I'm similar to all people in that I love to be inspired. I hate to be corrected, but I love to be inspired.) Tears of sadness because I know that I, myself, am not overcoming the way the person on the screen is. I myself am nurturing my obstacles. Gaining sympathy from them. I am crying because I am grieving for my lost life. A life lost to self-pity that could have been a life of joyful action.

My wife Kathy began a workout program. I was the one who was overweight, but she began going to the club to work out. Sometimes I'd go with her. Sometimes not. Her workout wasn't easy. Once I got on the same kind of machine she was on, right next to her, and tried to keep up with her for the full 40 minutes, working arms and legs like mad. I lasted about 10 minutes. "That's enough of this insanity," I thought.

I tried to bait her into judging me. I tried to get her to tell me that I needed the workouts more than she did. But she never took the bait.

"Of course, I want you to be healthy and happy, but you look great to me," she said. "Do what-ever you want to do, and don't push it."

And every day she set her alarm, woke up early, and worked out. Whether she felt like it or not. No comment on me, no judgment. Just an unintentional example to witness. Finally her example became inspiring to me so I got more and more serious. I began working out myself more and more often, and I started losing weight and adding some much-needed physical pride and energy to my life.

The truth is, Kathy never would have gotten me to change by critiquing and judging me. Just as Morey will never get the teachers around him to love their students by judging them. Because judgment is toxic to both parties—to the judge and the judged.

Kathy working out was Gandhi saying, "Be the change." Forget others. Stop trying to change them. They are not your problem. You are your problem. Change yourself. And then notice how much better others look to you.

Chapter 8

The Story of Growing Old

"The world is a spell, an enchantement, an amazement, an arabesque of such stunning rhythm and a plot so intriguing that we are drawn by its web into a state of involvement where we forget that it is a game."

—Alan Watts

I went to hear Dr. Andrew Weil give a talk a few nights ago about "Healthy Aging," and one of the things I found myself hoping would change was our society's story about old people.

The entire youth culture has turned contemporary movies into vulgar gross-out competitions and much modern music into obscene ranting. Even TV commercials aimed at the youth culture have become almost too childishly gross to endure. I watch with the remote control at the ready. Zap! I can't afford to have that commercial go into my head. Zap!

It's as if TV commercials and summer movies today are all written by naughty kids desperate to get attention. As ratings plunge and Hollywood suffers box-office slumps, the makers of TV commercials and summer movies become hungry for more shock value. Anything to appeal to young people.

Dr. Weil talked about the insanity of seeing every older actress and TV personality get radical plastic nip-and-tuck facial operations to "reverse" the aging process, as if aging were wrong and bad. When I see some of these actresses with their newly inflated lips, it appears as if they have been beaten about the face with a small baseball bat.

All in the name of avoiding aging, as if being old was awful.

Weil predicted this would change soon. He told us that the "baby boomer" generation, now entering senior status, would return focus and dignity to aging.

I found myself hoping he was right, because it's just a made-up story to say that young is better than old. It's not true. Some cultures revere their older people and treat them as wise and knowledgeable treasures. Is that *more* true? Maybe not. But it serves us better. It's a more beautiful and functional story. As long as we're going to tell a story, society benefits from a story that has beauty and function.

Weil said to us, "Why are old wines and whiskeys valued much more than young ones? Why are we moved in the presence of old trees? When you age cheese, it improves the cheese. Antiques are valuable *because* they are so old. Older violins are the most treasured."

Weil asked us to consider all the qualities of aging that make these things so much more valuable and be willing to apply them to people, too. In effect, to change the whole story we have about older people. As I listened to him, he made me think of something the columnist Mark Steyn had written. I laughed to myself as I remembered that Steyn wrote, "I like old people. I like old movies. I like old songs. I'll take 'Moonlight Becomes You' over 'Yo, Bitch! Sit on This!' any day."

In the story of King Arthur and the Knights of the Round Table, the aged wizard Merlin was the most powerful figure of all. His wisdom and spiritual gifts made him almost superhuman.

The next most powerful figure was King Arthur himself, older than his knights, and therefore wiser and a stronger character. This is just a story, but the usefulness of this story is profound. If we brought this story home, it could bring tremendous benefits to our own society.

Our society treats old age as though it's a sickness. As if we need all kinds of government programs for old people to get their shelves filled with pharmaceuticals, or else they will just drop dead (or not vote for you—even worse!).

But older people have learned great lessons about how to care for themselves. How to save money. How to be resourceful. Yet, we treat them otherwise, because that's the story we've created around them.

This negative aging story soon becomes con-vincing. It even entrances the old people themselves! Some older people, when they retire, start walking differently. They hobble and shuffle along. They speak differently, too, as if in a play with new parts to play. They stop exercising because their story is that they're old now. Their voices get high-pitched, thin, reedy, and weak. How much of that is the physical decline, and how much of it is living into the pre-scripted story?

The reality is that, these days, old people aren't as close to death as we think they are. Or as they think they are. Look at the quantum leaps here in life expectancy: (Table 8.1)

LIFE EXPECTANCY	Years
Cro-Magnon Era	18
Ancient Egypt	25
1400s Europe	30
1800s Europe and U.S.	37
1900s U.S.	48
2003 U.S.	78

Table 8.1

So if we can expect to live until 78, why do we retire at 65? What should we do for those 13 long years? (Live into the senior citizen story! Lobby for more and more pharmaceuticals.)

I'd like to tell different stories about old people. Maybe if we all tell enough contradictory stories, good things will start to happen. People might start living differently. I like to tell the story of the wonderful novelist Norman Maclean.

At the age of 73, Norman Maclean decided to reject the idea of going into a comfortable retirement. It would have been easy for him to do. He had taught literature at the University of Chicago for many years, and everyone told him he deserved a nice, restful retirement. But something was nagging him. In all the years that he *taught* literature, he wondered if he himself could have produced it. He wondered if he could have been a writer himself. He wondered. Most people wonder a lot about things such as that in their old age. But why just wonder?

Soon, Maclean got excited about the idea of writing. It was almost as if he took the great writer George Eliot's advice when she said, "It's never too late to be what you might have been." (The great novelist George Eliot's real name was Mary Ann Evans. But back in old England, the story was that you had to be a man to be taken seriously as a writer.)

Norman Maclean said he "decided to give up some of the things associated with happiness in old age like running around with women, travel, etc." Instead, he would find out if he could be a writer. He went to his cabin in Montana and, in a joyfully disciplined way, began to write. He soon realized that he had the same power a 20-year-old had. He had it right there in his heart and his two hands. He kept typing. He couldn't stop. He connected with his power to make up an entirely new story about himself.

Lo and behold! He was a wonderful writer! A true novelist! Two years later, he emerged from his cabin with his highly acclaimed masterpiece *A River Runs Through It.* It is a novel written with a passion and poetic fire normally only associated with bright, young talent.

It was simply *not true* that he was too old to become a writer. That was just a story. He wasn't willing to live into that story.

Yet I can't tell you how many people have told me that they "always wanted to" write, or act, or be a musician, or something along those lines, but that now, of course, it was a little late, because they were 30 or 40 or 50 years old.

I have 30-year-olds talking to me as if they are on their deathbeds.

"I'm too old for that," they say with a straight face.

That's their story, and they're sticking to it.

What have you told yourself you are too old to do? Are you too old to become an actor, maybe? John Housman started acting in his 70s and later won an Academy Award for his acting in *The Paper Chase.*

One of my own stories about aging was that I assumed I was too old to start writing books. I decided this up until the age of 49. I was nearly 50! My life had not been focused enough to allow me all the early discipline and dues-paying to ever be a writer of books. That was my story. My life had been chaotic. I was an alcoholic for some years, and even though I had gotten clean and sober, I had children to raise and my life was a wild, disjointed ride from job to job. How can anyone succeed at writing books with a life story such as that?

My response to that question was interesting. It was not focused or absolute, as Maclean's was. It was tentative and cowardly. What finally happened was a case of two stories colliding with each other. My own story of being "too old" didn't fit with my 16-year-old daughter Stephanie's story of "my dad is a good enough writer to get his book published." So Stephanie helped by sending out a number of samples of my writing. To my great surprise my first book got published. When two stories collide, the stronger story wins.

But now I had a dilemma. What was I to do with my "too old" story? It didn't seem to apply anymore. So, I simply stopped telling the story. To myself or anyone else. I began putting together a string of actions that let me create a new story, a flexible story that changed with every heartbeat. I would write and keep writing till my dying day. That was my new story. And I was making myself up as I went. Reinventing myself and motivating myself. No outside influences need apply. Circumstance not welcome. And I vowed to never let any one story stay there long enough to catch me up in its web. Stories will do that. They will seduce us. And then they'll do the ultimate nasty thing: they will lead us to believe them.

It took me many years to understand what Fichte meant when he said, "Being free is nothing. Becoming free is everything." Because "being free" is just another static story. "I'm free" is a story. Even though it sounds good, it won't last, because stories don't. There's nothing to them, so how could they last? But *becoming* free is not a story—it's an action! It's movement inside a journey. In fact, it's a glorious movement that takes you beyond time and space and into the dance of pure becoming.

Why should we deny old people that experience of pure becoming? Why should we put them in a story that says, "Shut up, sit down in your recliner, and take your meds. Feeling a little depressed that you're no longer useful or in action? Well, here's a little drug for that depression. Don't forget to vote. We'll drive you to the polls. Yes, our van is wheelchair-accessible! And so, from now on, if you feel any psychological discomfort about being an old person, we can just have your doctor take care of it for you. See ya, old-timer!"

At the age of 71, Woody Strong was diagnosed with inoperable cancer by medical specialists in Denver. He was informed that he only had one year to live. He had inoperable cancer. "Nothing we can do," he was told. But drugs. Take these drugs Woody. See ya, Woody! And because of the wonderful book on longevity and health called *Fantastic Voyage* by Ray

Kurzweil and Terry Holland, we know how the story of Woody Strong turned out.

After hearing the sad news, Woody thought he'd like to spend his last year in Nepal. He loved Nepal. He was loved there, too, for how much he and his wife Penny helped provide education and medical care for thousands of Nepali in the Himalayans. Many children there thought of him as a father, so dying in Nepal would be a nice final wish.

But upon arriving in Nepal, Woody's friends there convinced him not to accept his death warrant. They didn't buy the story that he had to die right now. They got him to visit a renowned healer in the remote Everest region of Nepal.

At first, Woody was very skeptical. Who was this healer? Hadn't the most modern doctors in Colorado already looked at every possibility? Didn't they say that their drugs were all he had for final comfort before the inevitable. Wasn't that right? Or not?

For the next five days, Woody Strong was led through an intensive healing ceremony. He laughed and cried and broke into enormous sweats "for no reason." At the end of the ceremony, the lama told Woody he was cured!

Cured? From terminal cancer? By laughing and crying and sweating?

When Woody Strong went back to Colorado months later, he was as astonished as his doctors were to learn that there was no sign whatsoever of cancer in him! Gone! Two stories had collided, and the healer's story prevailed. It was stronger. The lama and the ceremony healed Woody Strong.

***

When I was a boy, I used to love being with my grandfather Sam Chandler as we hiked across the southern Arizona desert, gathering rocks up to put in his tumbler to polish and smooth out and make things with. I loved hearing his stories about the old days in the west, in part because of how active and alive he was *now.* He could out-walk me by quite a bit. He had energy! He was still *becoming* someone. He wasn't stuck in a final, sealed-off story of who he was. He was excited about the lamps he was making from old cactus wood and polished rocks.

How old would you be if you didn't know how old you were? What if some quirk erased all your memory and dropped you in a little town on another continent to live? You had all your faculties, and you could start a new life. You just wouldn't know how old you were, or have a past to live up to (or be depressed about). How old would you be then?

Do you have an answer to that question?

Would you look into a mirror and try to figure it out? Would you be old? You can't be old unless you have a story about how old you are. You can't be world-weary unless you have a big, heavy story about all that has happened to you. What if someone erased the story?

Some people tell me that their story was not written by them, but by circumstance. Please don't tell me that. Don't tell me it's circumstance. Because there are deliriously happy people who have endured "horrific" circumstances. Just as there are bitterly depressed people who have been nurtured and well taken care of all their lives. Where's the cause and effect in those stories? Circumstance means nothing. Your story about the circumstance means everything. So if you didn't "know" how old you were, how old would you be?

Chapter 9

Converting Your Story Into a Fire

"I'll burn you like a candle, honey,
I'm going to burn you at both ends."

—Dinah Washington
"Evil Gal Blues"

Francis had called me because his national network of fruit basket salespeople were being undermined by one very nasty man-child named Rudy. Rudy was once one of Francis's top salespeople, but Rudy had defected and was now spreading bad rumors.

For example, he was calling and e-mailing all the other sales reps across the country and telling them that Francis's company was unfair and even illegal in the way it was set up. Rudy was also saying that Francis himself was a fraud and should not be trusted. There was new gossip. Rudy had it.

Francis called me in hysterics because of all this.

I said, "How can I help you, Francis?"

"Well, you always have ways of seeing things differently than I do, and I am in a real crisis right now. In fact, I've never had a crisis such as this in my business, and I don't know what to do about it."

I told Francis that if I was going to help him with this crisis, we had to first eliminate the word *crisis* from our conversation. I needed Francis to shut down and reboot. I don't encourage people to indulge in crises. It's too big a luxury. We can't afford it if we're going to thrive.

Francis said, "It's not a crisis? What else is it? You want me to engage in positive thinking at this point? Sorry, not appropriate! This guy is ruining my reputation!"

I reminded Francis (because we had talked many times before) that "crisis" was a perception and, therefore, his choice. He can perceive and describe things any way he wants, and to choose the most catastrophic and alarming, self-victimized language only disempowers him at a time when power is what he needs. The word *crisis* only makes him weak in the face of the "crisis." At that moment

Francis needed to be strong. Even stronger than usual.

Francis had to be reminded that the best way to deal with a problem is to overwhelm it. Unless he was willing to walk away from it and declare it a non-issue—which also works. But if he has decided to take the problem on, the best approach is absolute bone-crushing overwhelm. Full-metal, heavy metal, full-throttle overwhelming blitz. Nothing less.

Don't let the problem fester, Francis. Don't let Rudy keep spreading that poison without responding creatively.

(It took me many hard and painful years to learn a basic truth about problems in the workplace of life: *problems don't age well.* The longer a problem lives, the harder it gets to solve.)

Once I learned that Speed of Takedown was the most valuable measuring stick in problem-solving, everything got easier. The lawyer Marianne learned this lesson, and Francis could learn this, too: The minute you identify a problem, and I mean accurately identify it for what it is, BRING ALL YOU'VE GOT TO IT AS FAST AND AS FORCEFULLY AS YOU CAN

TO MASSIVELY OVERWHELM THE PROBLEM, AS THOUGH KILLING AN ANT WITH A SLEDGEHAMMER.

Move quickly. Be totally focused. Get other people to help. Don't let the subject be changed. How you solve this problem is how you solve your life, because how you do anything is how you do everything. Be massive. Overwhelm. Be energetic. Be excited. Be powerful. Be thorough. Be complete. And remember: better to solve it now than later. Problems don't age well.

Rudy was slandering Francis in a very malicious way (as disgruntled former employees sometimes do, to protect their humiliated stories) and Francis was not knowing what to do other than dance and fret. Dance around his house and call other people, and fret and squeal about it.

So he and I created a massive action plan. That's different than a regular action plan. It's massive. That's why we called it a massive action plan, which included lawyers, and FedEx, and "Cease and Desist" orders, e-mail campaigns, and rhetorical intimidation.

But I didn't want to stop there. I wanted to go further, so I asked Francis, "How can we take this situation and convert it into something great? How can we transform it into something that furthers your mission?"

Francis was confused. Francis was used to thinking about his crises as bad things. Make the bad thing go away! He never entered into inquiries about *using* "bad" things for the greater good. Because that's how stories work to trap us. That's how disempowering stories about bad things keep us spellbound. Once you've got a wounded victim story going about how you've been unfairly treated, you don't really want to change it. Victim stories are too good to change once you've invested time and imagination into them! Victim stories make you feel special. You are not common anymore. You're not a nonentity. You are special. You've been uniquely victimized. What a delicious ego trip. Even though it's negative, it's still a rush! You have been specially singled out by Rudy for mistreatment. You're right and Rudy's wrong. You're starting to look *good* here!

People tell victim stories to make themselves look good. If their boss has been unfair and unkind to them, they look good by comparison. A victim is a kind of reverse hero of the story. A martyr. Maybe even a saint. It's the secret payoff.

But Francis was having none of that kind of analysis. He was impatient with my concepts. It sounded too much like nonsense to him. He wanted to stay with how bad this all was. I hung in there, because I wanted to show Francis another way to go, another possible story that had the Rudy experience strengthen—not weaken—the mission of Francis's company.

"How could something this bad strengthen the mission?" asked Francis.

I asked Francis if he was royally ticked off. Really furious? Full of righteous anger? Rip-roaring mad?

"Yes!" he said.

"Good! Let's use that marvelous energy, not waste it. Let's use it to build something with. Let's use it to communicate with. Let's cut a CD and a voice-mail message right now, right when you're still feeling this, for all your sales reps all across America about what has happened and how you are not going to take it anymore. You're mad as heck! Let's have you shout to them in no uncertain terms how this company was formed, on passion and integrity and vision! Let them feel it. Shake them up. Make even bolder promises to them than you have ever made before. Step up to this. Use it. Use it for fuel. Go wild."

Francis got excited. Now he was psyched. Now he was directed and focused. Now he couldn't wait to rush into the little recording studio he used and put together a furious, bold CD for all his people.

In the months that followed, sales went up at Francis's company. Francis said that the "incident" solidified his company and was thought of now as a blessing.

"Amazing how you can use 'adversity' and build on it," he said.

And this illustrates not only how powerful stories are, but how they can be rewritten and turned into something completely different for the higher good.

Sometimes when trouble shows up in my life I like to think about a log in the road. I might first see the log in the road as an obstacle. Rudy calling people and lying about Francis was an "obstacle." At first glance, a log. But a log is also something you can put on a fire. What happens when you put a log on the fire? It gets consumed, for one thing. But what else? By being consumed, it makes the fire stronger, brighter, and hotter. The log actually feeds the fire!

Obstacles feed the mission!

That's why it's so important to face problems with a fire in your heart. Not to tiptoe around problems, but once the decision is made to encounter the problem, to light your internal fire and go after it. Consume it. Convert it into energy. It changes the story of the log when you put it on the fire. And then it changes the story of you.

Chapter 10

Is There Time to Win This Thing?

"So many different people to be."

—Donovan
"Season of the Witch"

I recently attended a writer's workshop put on by the popular mystery author Lawrence Block. Writers in the audience asked him, "What about time management? How do you find time to write?"

He was cruel, but honest, in his response. He said that if you're not writing, it's simply because you don't want to write. There are things you *are* doing that you'd rather do. And if you don't *want* to write, why bother with time management anyway? Why bother with a writer's workshop, even? When you have something in your life you really want to do, you don't have to "find" time, because you'll already have made time. You're already doing it.

It occurred to me as I was sitting in the audience that he was right. I mean, a lot of people winced and said "ouch" when he said it because it hurt them to realize that they were not writing because they really didn't want to write, even though their story was different. Their story was that they would *love* to be writers but the realities of daily life and responsibilities made that next to impossible.

That was not a true story!

For years, pop-fiction author James Patterson *(Along Came A Spider)* had a very demanding career at J. Walter Thompson advertising agency. Yet during that very busy time, he also began his career as a writer of pop fiction.

How did he "find the time" to write while working in an industry as all-consuming as advertising?

Patterson said he loved to do it, so it was never a problem. He would just discipline himself to get up every morning around 4:30 and then write until 6:00. The rest of the day was for his other, normal life.

"I think if you love to do something, you find a way to do it," Patterson said in an online interview with *Reader's Digest.* "The nice thing for me is that fiction writing has never been a job, and it still isn't. It's always been an escape. When I go into a bookstore and see a novel by some author that I really like, I feel that sense of excitement, and that's what I feel every day when I sit down to write. It's the same heart-pumping 'I can't wait to just see how today's installment turns out!' feeling."

In my work consulting and coaching people who want more professional success, I have found that this illusion of "not finding enough time" also prevails. People don't understand that the whole "time management" problem is really no problem at all. Many sales teams and leadership teams come to me for "time management" training when time management is not the issue. (How do you manage time, anyway? Can you jam more than 24 hours into a day?)

Time is not the problem. Focused intention is the problem. Desire is the problem. High levels of desire generate focus and commitment and soon people are *making* time for their project. Just as James Patterson did.

So I just sat there in that writer's workshop listening to Lawrence Block tell us that, if we weren't finding enough time to write, it meant we didn't want to write. I reminded myself that this is true of anything I want to do. I want to remind myself every day (every day!) that time is *made,* not found. (It's always available.)

Henry Davenport said, "The great dividing line between success and failure can be stated in five words: *I did not have time."*

So why do we compose stories about time that aren't true?

Maybe it's because we are all writers of fictional lives, beginning with who we think we are, and then proceeding on to our limitations. The story of our lives soon becomes the story of our limitations.

Sometimes, to make the story feel better, we make *other people* responsible for those limitations. Stories that have a villain in them are always more fun to tell. It's traditional! (Sometimes we even say God is responsible.)

"Suppose that you were living your life," psychologist Harald Graning said, "and all of a sudden God came down and destroyed your house? You'd probably be pissed."

However! If you will rent and watch the movie *Lawrence of Arabia,* you'll get an insight into how fast a dysfunctional story can be erased.

In *Lawrence of Arabia,* there was an unforgettable scene in which T.E. Lawrence's army had just gone through a difficult 10-day march through the desert. The soldiers were near death from dehydration when they found a pool of water and happily jumped in. Later, when Lawrence took a head count of his men, he noticed that one of the camel boys was missing. They found the boy's empty camel near the back of the camp and concluded that he must have fallen off during the sandstorm.

"We must go back and find him," Lawrence shouted to his men. But his men refused to go back into the brutal sandstorm.

"Master," they begged, "it is Allah's will that the boy did not return with us. His fate was written by God. We must not interfere."

Lawrence angrily mounted his camel and headed back into the desert sandstorm by himself. His men stood there, shaking their heads in bewilderment. "Now we've lost *him,* too," they said, as they returned to the comfort of the oasis. Two days later an iridescent image emerged from the heat wave. "It's Lawrence!" the men shouted. "He has found the boy!" They ran eagerly to assist him. Lawrence leaned over and handed them the boy, who was unconscious but alive and well. He looked into their eyes and said in a raspy whisper, "Remember this: nothing is written unless *you* write it."

Lawrence said in his memoirs, "All men dream: but not equally. Those who dream by night in the dusty recesses of their minds wake in the day to find that it was vanity: but the dreamers of the day are dangerous men, for they may act out their dream with open eyes, to make it possible."

For a child, that's the whole glory of life, because the child is still connected to his essence of pure spirit, energy, and joy. He or she can turn into anyone. On the spot.

My 5-year-old grandson makes up stories and roles for people to play. On Halloween night (the season of the witch) we were sitting together at a table in my kitchen and he picked up a straw figurine of a witch and said to me, "You be the witch."

I started talking in my *Wizard of Oz* witch voice to him, and then asked him, "Who are *you* going to be?"

And as I looked into his eyes I could see by how they sparkled that he was doing an internal scan. He was deciding who to be. And I could tell by his happiness that the list to choose from was infinite.

Soon that list will grow smaller for him. Part of my job as his crazy grandfather will be to keep him aware of how many people he can be.

As civilization attempts to age us, we start (in self-defense) writing the story of who we are—or, who we think we darn well *better be* to survive these things called death and taxes and a demanding family. We feel that we better make up exactly who we are. We better assign our limitations. We might want to banish joy to the future. Banish it for now. Just for now. We don't deserve it yet. We haven't "made it." We better tell ourselves we'll allow ourselves to feel joy when certain conditions are met. When our home is paid off. When this career gets off the ground. When I meet that certain someone. When the Cubs win the World Series (or is it just get there?). Joy is in the future and, I guess, happiness is in the past.

"Are you happy?"

"No."

"Were you ever happy?"

"Oh yes, once." (Music from *Camelot* rises.)

We also put the burden of happiness and joy on outside agents, such as sports teams. Such as the Cubs! We cheer for our teams to *make it* and get some national recognition, because we think that will add to our own story. We forget we can write our story. We forget that nothing is written until we write it. So, having forgotten this, we try to add the glory of the team to our own resume.

"How's Steve?"

"Really happy."

"Why?"

"The University of Arizona won the tournament, and you know he went to school there, and so he's on cloud nine."

Let's probe that further. Okay? Let's find out what the story is with this fanaticism. (The word *fan* comes from the word *fanatic.*)

"Why does that U. of A. victory make him so happy? Did he bet money?"

"Oh, no, he uses the team as a surrogate. You know how there are surrogate fathers? He uses the team as a surrogate achiever. If they achieve something great, because he went to the school and wears all the blue and red Wildcat gear (when they're playing well, when they're not he puts it in the closet and tells people he doesn't follow the team all that much anymore), if they achieve something great, he pulls that aura into him. He cups his hands and waves it into his own system. That's what he does with his team's success. He gets high on it. Then he adds it to his story. It becomes part of his story. It's a way for him to win without doing anything but cheering—oh my, he yells his lungs out. He yells and curses at the games. Because his story is at stake. All his friends on the East Coast? They are watching the results of this game and they know that Steve is a real die-hard fan."

"Die-hard? That's a strange phrase."

"You know what it means, though. It's a thing that doesn't die easily. It dies hard. It's hard to kill! You can't kill it! That's the beauty of building up your story. If you have a strong enough story, you build a buffer against death. How could someone that successful at living die?"

"It would be hard!"

"Right. So it's as if he should be carrying a sign at the games that says PLEASE WIN THIS FOR ME!"

"Or maybe, I CAN'T, BUT MAYBE YOU CAN!"

"Yes! Go out there and live life for me in these next two hours and WIN IT ALL! For me. And your other fans."

That's why when the team wins the "big one," they come home to the airport and they see huge throngs of people welcoming them. And, invariably, there is a sign, a huge sign that is being held up by a group of people that says "THANK YOU."

"Thanks for doing what I can't do."

But we are really confused to think that. Because there are *so many* things we can do that our athlete heroes can't do. So many wonderful, touching, human life skills that they do not have. Yet we get confused and think that they are "winning" and we are not.

For example, many people die (literally!) during and after world soccer matches. That's how invested they are in their teams playing *for them.* Living life and challenging what's possible *for them.*

And it's not just happening in foreign lands. I recently heard football coach Terry Bowden on a sports talk radio show say that the Auburn-Alabama rivalry was so great that each year there was "at least one trailer park death" after the big game. He sounded proud.

GO TEAM!: Play for me. Live for me. Add to my story!

Sports are fun. For me, they are one of the great joys in life. And I do have teams I cheer for, including my beloved Arizona Wildcats. But it's important that I don't start confusing things. That I don't try to enhance my own identity by leeching success from the team. Being a fan is fun when I know how to keep it playful. It's a game, I remind myself. Just a game. The real danger of confusion comes from making the outcomes of the games important to my story, and then of making my story important to my happiness.

Chapter 11

Attack of the Resume Enhancers

"The most costly of all follies is to believe passionately in the palpably not true."

—H.L. Mencken

It would be great if we could plant a chip in everyone's head (and maybe in the future we will) that sends the brain a simple message each morning when people wake up and go out into the world.

The message would say, "You're already enough."

It would mean that people could be confident of their power. They could reach deep inside for what they needed and know that they always had enough in there to get the job done.

The chip would not only give them confidence, it would lead them to more and more growth. They would enjoy the fun of increasing their skills and depth, because the chip would ground them every day in a starting block that says they're already enough. They would be certain that they had access to enough resources inside them for anything and everything important.

This chip would be a breakthrough, because most people don't start from that place. In fact, most people I know and work with start from "I'm *not enough.*"

And then, while thinking they're *not enough,* they chase strange rainbows and inflate their personal, biographical stories along the way. They pump up their resumes with some extreme-ly insane additions! All in the name of a better story. A story that makes them finally seem to be "enough."

Consider the governor of New Mexico, Bill Richardson. You would think his life story was already enough! He's been mentioned as a potential presidential candidate! He's a governor. He was our UN ambassador! What a big success! What more would he want?

Well, he is now acknowledging that his longtime claim to have been drafted to play for the Kansas City Athletics (now the Oakland A's) in 1966 while a right-handed pitcher at Tufts University has been less than truthful. And it's not that he realized, all by himself, that this untruthfulness was not a good or necessary thing. No. He did not come forward voluntarily. The *Albuquerque Journal* had to check out his lifelong "drafted by the major leagues" claim to find it empty. He was never drafted by anyone. Ever.

Richardson had a strangely unconscious response when he was confronted with this artificial enhancement of his resume. He said, "After being notified of the situation and after researching the matter ... I came to the conclusion that I was not drafted by the A's." How very odd that language is.

Richardson explained that he was scouted by several major league teams in the 1960s. He said his name appeared on "a draft list of some kind" created by the Los Angeles Dodgers and Pittsburgh Pirates. He named team scouts, now dead, who he said told him that he "would or could" be drafted.

And that's often the otherworldly logic of resume enhancers: "If I *could* have been drafted, then why can't I say I *was* drafted?"

A teammate of Richardson's at Tufts rushed to his defense when the story came out. Paul

Barry wrote to the Albuquerque newspaper saying, "I believe the baseball draft story is an accurate description of his baseball ability."

So the story's not true but it's an accurate description. Not true but accurate! Paul Barry is suggesting if he had the *ability* to be drafted, then it's okay for him to put it in his resume. I mean he was that good! He *could* have been drafted, as good as he was! Why not just put it in there?

The real reason Richardson put it in his resume is because he didn't believe he was *enough* without it. Of course, he was enough, he was more than enough without the fabrication, but he didn't believe it. He has since proven that he is enough, but he didn't believe it back when he crafted his first story about himself.

Harmless? Maybe. But pathetic nonetheless. In many ways we are all Bill Richardson. We live in fear that our stories won't be enough. So we keep adding to them. Sometimes we add real, true things to our stories. New boats and new homes and new cars and new spouses and new travels. Those are real things. You can look at them and say, "Hey, check me out! Look at all my new stuff!"

I know a woman who believes the fact that she has lived in many different places, and even to this day lives part of the year in different places, adds depth to her story. She's always talking about the various exotic places she's been, and when she writes she always puts a big byline at the top, signaling the impressive exotic place she's writing from. What she hasn't confronted is that no matter where she goes, it's still her that's there. All her pompous miseries go with her everywhere. Everywhere she goes, there she is! She can't change that. And the very people she tries to impress with her foreign datelines and post-marks are shaking their heads and laughing at her. Because they see the transparency of the attempt she is making to add to her "not enough" belief. We can often see this human folly quite clearly in others. It's really graphic and gross in the resume enhancers. We're even a little embarrassed for them. Because we can also identify with that feeling of not yet being enough.

But in the end, even these resume enhance-ments don't do much to help the constant nagging feeling that our lives are not enough. So sometimes we go even further. And some of us ramp up the biographical fiction.

Governor Richardson's little lie was not as ramped-up as the resume enhancement done by Notre Dame's head football coach a few years ago, George O'Leary.

Actually, George O'Leary was only coach at Notre Dame for five days. He resigned almost as soon as he was hired, admitting he lied about his academic and athletic background. (But only after some journalists checked his resume against the facts.) O'Leary had claimed to have a master's degree in education and to have played college football for three years. But checks into his background showed these claims were not true.

A master's degree from New York University in 1972? Not really. O'Leary *was* a student there, but did not receive a degree. Three years of playing football? In fact, his school, New Hampshire, reports that he never played in a game. Not one down of football.

O'Leary said he regretted not telling Notre Dame officials about the "inaccuracies" before he was hired.

But this is a strange choice of words, here: *inaccuracies.* Because these are not just inaccuracies. These are deliberate fictions. So the distortion continues. Imagine the pain of the person who must continue to distort things even after being found out.

When you regret having made an "inaccuracy" it simply means you got something wrong. Maybe you said you spent $129 and you spent $122. That would be an inaccuracy. Inaccuracies are also considered to be unintentional.

O'Leary also tried to float to the public the possibility that these "inaccuracies" were actually caused by a convergence of *good* things, admirable things about him that had come together to issue forth these inaccuracies. Notre Dame officials said O'Leary had left campus and returned to Atlanta. In a subsequent statement released by the university, O'Leary further discussed his decision to resign:

"Many years ago, as a young married father, I sought to pursue my dream as a football coach," he said, calling forth an almost saintly image of himself. "In seeking employment I prepared a resume that contained inaccuracies regarding my completion of course work for a master's degree and also my level of participation in football at my alma mater. These misstatements were never stricken from my resume or biographical sketch in later years."

Never stricken from the record? Who forgot to strike those from the record? Was the record-striker on strike? Was he saying they *would* have been stricken had he known they were there? Was he suggesting that the lies were just booster rockets for his career that were meant to be discarded once they got him off the ground?

This scrambling is sad to watch. A newly twisted story being quickly assembled to replace a false story. Even while fessing up to the false nature of his story, O'Leary was quickly telling another. Because this one seemed to be a better, truer, more heartwarming story to replace it with. He wanted us to know, because it wasn't in his earlier story, that he was "a young married father." He was hoping we would think those were touching new story elements. Add to that a dream he had of being a football coach. And don't these righteous, moral drives and passions sometimes produce inaccuracies?

Come on, George, you just lied! Just say so and get on with your resignation!

The forced resignation of O'Leary was one of the most embarrassing blows ever to the storied Notre Dame football program, famous for

Rockne, Leahy, the Four Horsemen, and winning one "for the Gipper."

Next, Notre Dame athletic director Kevin White attempted a classic minimizing statement intended to muffle the embarrassment. The way you run over to help mop up a drink spilled by a drunken relative. White said O'Leary acknowledged "problems" in O'Leary's biographical materials, "including his academic background. And I understand that these inaccuracies represent a very human failing; nonetheless, they constitute a breach of trust that makes it impossible for us to go forward with our relationship," White said.

A very human failing indeed. We humans fail to see that we are enough. That's a human failing.

And it's amazing how the media will rush to try to convert a villain into a victim. (Our society, by the way, dictates what the media does by what kind of news it likes to buy or watch. So it's easy and popular to blame "the media" for all kinds of moral failings, but the media is simply trying to anticipate what will get ratings and readers.) Look at how George O'Leary is now treated, now that he has taken the University of Central Florida on to a major winning season. (Note on that winning season: O'Leary is a fantastic football coach. Even better than his false resume said he was!)

After O'Leary had a great season with Central Florida, the headline writers wrote: "Much Maligned Coach Redeems Self in Bowl Game." Maligned? What do they mean by maligned? Do they know what maligned means? Maligned means, according to the dictionary, that someone has said "false and unpleasant things about someone or to unfairly criticize them."

What's false and unpleasant about saying that someone had a human failing that resulted in inaccuracies in his resume? In fact, that's not maligning at all—that's closer to a codependent cover-up.

Yet, look at how the story has grown! Now the story around O'Leary is that he was once a maligned, poor guy, and he had to struggle his way back up the ladder by coaching at Central Florida and winning there.

Here's what's sad about all this storytelling. What's sad is that O'Leary is really a terrific football coach. Certainly good enough to have taken over at Notre Dame. At Central Florida he engineered the top program turnaround in the nation. After going 0–11 in 2004, UCF went 8–4 in 2005, including a 7–1 regular-season mark in their conference. Even more remarkable, UCF did it with a roster filled with freshmen and sophomores.

O'Leary has got what it takes! He's got enough coaching talent to not need a resume at all. Just look at how his teams play! Make up your own story around that!

I most admire the resume enhancement of actress Teri Garr. She talked about her life as a successful movie and TV actress recently on a television talk show.

There was a time in her early career when she was a dancer but wanted to transition into acting. Teri Garr admits that to get that shot, she listed on her resume roles she never had.

"I figured once I got in the door, they'd hire me immediately," Garr said. "But they're not gonna let me in the door unless I have a good headshot and a good resume. So I put in the resume a few things that looked better, like *Desire Under the Elms* on Broadway and a few credits. And then on the side of it was an asterisk. And at the bottom of the page of the asterisk I put '*LIE.'"

But no one speed-reading the resume noticed the asterisk or the word *LIE* at the bottom of the page. And if they had, what would it immediately mean to them? So in a technical way, Teri Garr maintained her integrity while inflating her resume.

Now here's the scary part: To some degree we all do a version of this. We polish our story up a little. Do I, too? Even me? Well, now that you mention it, yes. Here's an example I'm not proud of: I have often, in the past, in my little bios that I supplied to people who were thinking of hiring me, referred to myself as an "award-winning journalist." I'd string it in there with my past list of professions, all true, that included songwriter and advertising creative director. But was that award-winning journalist part really true? Yes, it was! In fact I didn't have any problem leaving it in the bio until my wife, Kathy, stumbled upon it one day and began asking me questions.

"Were you an award-winning journalist?" she asked.

"Yes," I said, not convincingly.

"Really, because I thought you were a sportswriter."

"That's a journalist," I said. "Can't a sportswriter be a journalist and get an award?"

"Sure, but what award did you win?"

"Oh, it was long ago...."

"Ha! This sounds fishy to me. People don't forget awards."

"I did get one! It's just that..."

"What? I knew there was a catch."

"Well, it was an award. Why can't we leave it at that? Why is one award any better or worse than any other award?"

"An award from where?"

"From a high school," I said, a little too softly.

Kathy began laughing. "From a *high school?*"

"I don't see the humor in that. You're laughing, but I worked hard as a journalist and this high school in Tucson. I was working the high school sports beat at the time ... and this high school presented me with an award for my writing."

"Oh, so you think that *counts* and should be listed on your professional bio?"

"Of course it counts! It's an award, isn't it? And it was given to me, right?"

"Was there a lot of competition for this award? I mean, how many other top journalists were up for this award? How many people in Tucson covered high school sports?"

"A few. Not a lot. Some."

"Fake!"

"What do you mean?"

"It's a fake and a deception to say you're an award-winning journalist because of that! I can't believe I married someone like you! You've got to stop saying that."

"Okay, okay, I'll leave it out! Gee!"

"You were making it sound as if you had won the Pulitzer or the Nobel Prize or something."

"Did I *say* 'Pulitzer'? Did I ever imply it?"

"No, but you were really stretching it."

"Okay, okay, who needs it?"

"You thought you did, obviously."

Actually, okay, I was probably wrong to do that. It lacked integrity. Not on the O'Leary scale or even the Richardson scale, but still, I admit it. To the world.

Maybe I could have said this to Kathy: "I was a young married father with a dream when I made a mistake based on the inaccuracies that occur whenever we exhibit a very human failing."

The truth, though? I inflated my story. Filled it up as though it was a balloon with hot air.

It's amazing how we try to keep adding to these stories of ours when we are already enough, and even *more than enough* to get the job done. To excel, even. Governor Richardson is widely admired for what he can do. George O'Leary is really a wonderful football coach. And Teri Garr is a charming comedic actress. The inflation wasn't necessary. The power was already there.

So go find where you've written down the story of you. It may be in your resume or in a bio you send around. Make sure it's true. And if the bare facts don't say enough about what you *can do,* then find another way to say so.

When you apply for a job, don't just let your resume speak for you. Go beyond that. Get really powerful letters of reference. Let your references pour their hearts out about you.

(If you are similar to most people, you have a problem remembering how good you really are. Couple that with how you were taught not to brag or be arrogant, and soon you have a real problem of misperception. You then confuse giving up your power with humility. Often it takes an outside voice, a friend or therapist or coach to counter the inner voice that says "I am not enough.")

Then tell your future employers what they can count on from you. *Show* them who you are by the enthusiastic, creative way you apply, and interview, and thank them for the interview.

No resume can compare to the power and joy of the *real you* in action. Give them a sample of some of that action.

Recently a company contacted me to say that it was considering hiring me to do a major training and coaching project with its people.

"We're looking at a few different consultants, so will you send us your brochure and a video?"

"I could. But I wouldn't want you to make your decision based on that, so let's get together."

"Okay, we'll book lunch."

"Lunch? Do you want to see how I eat lunch? What I order? My manners? Whether I salt my food before tasting it? No, I would rather not do lunch. The only time I do lunch is if my client owns a restaurant."

"What do you have in mind?"

"Experience. Action. Reality."

"What do you mean by that?"

"I'll come in and talk to a handful of your people for 20 minutes with you there, and then you can make your decision based on your experience of me and the actions I took to change your people's perspective. You can supplement that with talking to others who have worked with me."

"No video? No brochure?"

"I don't really have them."

So when he agrees to my visit, my only mission is to go in there and *show* what I can do. Much better than having them pore over my resume and bio to see if my story was a better story than my competitor's story.

There is power beyond the story. If we can step outside our stories and *perform* for people, we accelerate our success.

Do you see how that company that was thinking about hiring me was trapped in its addiction to stories? Rather than experience me in person, they wanted to see some stories (brochures, videos, and so forth) and then compare them to see if they matched up to their own stories about their need for coaching and training. There's no experience in that process.

Sometimes I do personal career coaching with individuals, and it's funny to me how they all want to see the Website, look at the fees, and read the testimonials. But no one thinks to ask for an experience. I like to give the experience itself and have them choose based on that.

I'm not trying to pass myself off as a superior being because I do this. It took me a long time to learn to do this—a long time to realize that stories are limited compared to real life, real love, and real enthusiastic performance. Stories are straightjackets and we are all dancers.

Once, years ago, my wife, Kathy, before she was my wife, wanted very badly to work for Nordstrom. They were opening a new store in Arizona, and hundreds and hundreds of women applied for sales positions because it was the first Nordstrom ever in Arizona, and Nordstrom, at the time, was the classiest of all department stores.

At first, Kathy worried about her resume. It wasn't enough. It showed no sales experience. No department store experience. Not that she would ever inflate it. She was the opposite of me in that regard. So I knew when we talked about it that our goal was to get her beyond her story and into the truth of whether she was really enough, and how she could prove it.

"Would you do a good job for them?" I asked.

"Yes, I think I'm perfect. I learn fast, I love talking to people, I'm passionate about clothing and fashion, I have energy, I..."

"Okay, okay, then the job is yours!" I said. "You got the job!"

"How do you mean? Why would they hire me? I have no retail sales experience. I've been a legal assistant and an editor at the State Bar. That's not the right profile for someone selling dresses."

"Maybe not, but *you* are perfect for them, and that's all that matters. Now the job is to sell yourself in such a way that the resume doesn't matter. Let your resume show you are educated, and a successful, loyal employee, but let's not focus on it. It's too limiting."

So Kathy sprung into action. She not only submitted her resume, but also a wonderful letter about why she wanted to work at Nordstrom, including stories about how she used to fly to California just to spend a day at Nordstrom there! Her letter was full of charm and energy and love for the profession. It caught the attention of the people hiring, and she was asked in for an interview.

In her interviews Kathy was just Kathy, full of enthusiasm about how much she wanted to work there and how much she loved the store and what a perfect match the profession was for her passions. After each interview, she asked herself how she could go the extra mile and separate herself from the others looking for that job—the others who had a better "story" about how they've worked retail clothing sales for years.

So Kathy was aggressive and creative in her follow-up to the interviews. She hand-delivered nice, long, handwritten notes of thanks, with specific references to the content of the interview and a very important extra compo-nent: Kathy told them *what they could count on* if they hired her.

That extra promising touch came out of a conversation we had about why people hire one person over another.

Kathy said, "I think they want someone ma-ture and adult enough to trust. So they don't have to manage them, emotionally, all day.

People they can actually count on to do the job."

"That's right!" I said. "You've got the key factor to getting hired! So be that for them. Be the one they can count on."

"But how?"

"By declaring it. By making bold promises to them that you can back up."

So Kathy got excited and sat down to write to the people she had interviewed with. Her letters told them *what they could count on* if they hired her. She boldly listed her promises of excellence and professional performance, and told them that these were commitments and they could count on them happening if she was hired.

She followed up with calls and further notes. And then she was called in just days after delivering those last letters and was hired. Hundreds of other applicants, with "better" resumes, were not hired.

Imagine Governor Bill Richardson being simply okay with who he was. Imagine him *not* putting on his bio that he was drafted by a major league baseball team out of college. Just leaving it off. Just imagine that one day, while running for governor, a bunch of journalists doing a feature on him follow him to a ball field, where he playfully takes the mound to offer up a few pitches to the local high school players during practice. One player after another strikes out! One player after another goes back to the dugout shaking his head yelling, "Who *is* this guy?!?!"

That would make an even better story than his inflated resume because it was real life happening outside of any prewritten story. It is action.

Imagine George O'Leary being interviewed for the big coaching position at Notre Dame with a truthful resume lying on the table in front of him. Imagine his interviewer, the president of the university, saying, "George, I don't see anywhere on your resume where you played college football. Do you expect us to hire you if you never played the game at the college level?"

O'Leary would say, "That's right. I never could play this game all that well. It was such a struggle for me to play that I had to learn everything the hard way. I had to learn things that other people could do naturally, without thinking. So now, what I *can do* is coach this game. If it's a coach you're looking for, there's no one who can do a better job for you. If you want a player, I'm not your guy."

I'd have hired him.

Chapter 12

The Power of Conscious Creation

"You have to be taught to hate and fear.
It has to be drummed in your dear little ear."

—South Pacific

You will remember that, in the famous musical *South Pacific,* a young American soldier fell in love with a girl of the South Sea Islands.

His love kept him from adopting any of the prevailing prejudice against "dark-skinned people" that other white people were demonstrating at the time. His story was a love story. But sooner or later the other people showed up with their own stories about different races and different stereotypes and, as the great song pointed out, these stories of prejudice are stories you have to be taught. They don't arise naturally.

Prejudice is nothing more than a negative story made up by people to give them a sense of advantage. They feel that diminishing someone else's story strengthens their own.

"One good thing about me is that I'm not one of them."

But stories can also be constructed for the good. Once the true power of stories is understood, stories can be used *positively* to move a good purpose along. A story has the power to do that. A compelling story can be likened to nuclear power, in a way. Used for evil, it's very destructive; used for good, it can light and warm a whole city.

My friend Burton in New York called because his company was having trouble with a few part-time workers who weren't really working the hours they said they would. It was just a few that were putting down more time than they were working, but enough to cause Burton alarm.

Most of his people were honorable and their time sheets could be trusted. But he now had enough delinquents to cause him concern.

He decided to put in a time clock at his office, so there would be an accurate, tangible record of his people's comings and goings from work.

But he was worried about the message it would send.

"I'm afraid it will look as though I no longer trust my people if I put the time clock in," Burton said. "So I'm not sure if I should do it."

"Well if you just do it, what will they think?" I asked.

"They'll think this is getting like a factory around here where no one is trusted."

"You're probably right!" I said.

"So, you're saying I shouldn't do the time clock."

"No, I'm not saying that."

Burton and I talked for a long time about the time clock because I wanted him to see that he had power to shape things. It was a power he didn't realize he had. The time clock being put in didn't have any real meaning by itself. (Nothing has "meaning" by itself until someone shows up to attach a story to it.) If he just put the clock in, his employees would add their own meaning to the event, and it would most likely be the very negative meaning that Burton worried about.

So why not see that the clock, in this suspended, perfect moment, has no meaning? Not without storytellers around. It means nothing at all. It's just a time clock sitting there.

When people can move into the present moment of awareness—the moment that elicits what the Samurai warriors call "no mind"—they can see the neutrality of all worldly things. And then, from there, if they choose to, they can create a story.

Could Burton create such a story? Could he create the meaning of the time clock before the event even happened? Yes he could. That's the power of a story when you consciously create it. Burton can use the power of a story to create thinking that's powerful and beguiling, and accomplishes what he wants.

"I'm not sure what I want," said Burton.

"Why do you want the time clock there, and how would you *like* them to respond to it?"

"I want it there to give us a more accurate accounting of who's working and who's not and—in truth?—who's cheating us. But not just that. Because it has occurred to me, too, that there are a lot of people who do the opposite. Who pop in and do something without recording their time. Just to get the job done. So I'd want everyone to just use the clock without losing any positive feelings they have for working here."

This was good to hear. Burton had clarity in his intention. If he could crystallize all his intentions in the workplace with that kind of precision, he would have a laser coming out of his office and his company would really be functional. I suggested to Burton that he tell his people just what he told me.

"Okay, okay," said Burton. "That all sounds great and all, but how do I do this without them resenting it?"

I suggested to Burton that he tell a story. A true story, but a story nonetheless.

I suggested that he talk about how the company is growing fast, "because of how good we have become and how much our clients love us, and how we aren't the tiny little team we used to be, so we need to keep responding to our growth by adding efficiencies and systems as we go, to keep track of our activities. You guys are in and out of here so often and in so many ways, the old systems are not keeping up with the activity, so I'm putting in automated time tracking. We'll see how it goes. See how you like it once you get used to it. So many of you are working so hard I don't want to lose even a minute of your contribution to us. This automated system will capture your work to the minute, so you're never shorted. Some of you jump in here to do something you forgot for a few minutes and don't put it on your card. I know you do. But never again. We're growing now, and I want you honored and compensated for it. And any other ideas you have where we can automate and get more high-tech, let me know!"

When Burton starts to see the power of pre-emptive, created communications, he'll shape his office buzz accordingly. Things happen, but they mean nothing until people add the meaning. If you can stay out in front of the storytelling curve, in a family or in a company, you can shape more events so that they flow in a purposeful direction.

Speaking of family, I had a friend once who worked with me in an advertising agency who intuitively knew the power of preemptively creating a story. Vic was about to announce to his children that he and their mother were going to be divorced.

One night, the night he was going to tell them, as I was packing up my things to leave the building, I noticed the light was still on in his office down the hall.

I asked Vic what he was doing.

"I'm creating a storyboard," he said.

"Who's the client?" I asked.

"My kids," he said.

As I moved into his office and looked more closely, I could see that Vic had made a huge whiteboard filled with family pictures with lines drawn from the pictures down to his three kids at the bottom.

"What is this all about?" I asked.

"These are the lines of love," he said. "I want my kids to see all the people in the family who love them and will always be there for them, loving them, with Mom and Dad right up there, never changing even after this divorce, never changing."

I was touched by how much heart and creativity Vic was putting into his family meeting. Given that the divorce was somewhat inevitable, I felt that his kids were lucky to have a father who would take the time to tell it this way.

I wished that his wife and he might have repaired their own partnership together, but, as the song by George Jones and Tammy Wynette said, they lived in a "two-story house." He had his story and she had hers.

So, for his children, Vic created the best story available to him at the time. It was true. It was sad. But it was loving and powerful.

Samuel Clemens was a great storyteller, too. He even made up a character in his life for himself to play called Mark Twain. Mark Twain knew a lot about how lives change when stories change, and wrote beautifully about the story of racism being replaced by the story of a child's love in *Tom Sawyer.* (For racism to even occur to you, you have to be carefully taught.)

Another story within a story jumps out in my memory of *Tom Sawyer.* It was the story of Tom's painting of the fence.

Tom Sawyer had to paint a fence one day with whitewash, and it was a chore he dreaded. The immediate automatic story was going to be, *Poor Tom, he has to paint a fence!* Ha ha ha ha. But Tom (and Mark Twain) knew how to alter the meaning of events. So Tom started telling his friends about how much *fun* it was to paint. How it was better than fishing or anything else. And the story got so good, his friends ended up begging Tom to let them finish whitewashing the fence.

Tom stepped back from this adventure with some newfound wisdom about life. He decided it wasn't such a meaningless world, after all. He had discovered a great law of human action, without knowing it—namely, that "in order to make a man or a boy covet a thing, it is only necessary to make the thing difficult to attain." At that point, Mark Twain adds his own observation: "Work consists of whatever a body is *obliged* to do, and Play consists of whatever a body is not obliged to do."

Tom Sawyer and the fence-painting story-within-a-story have endured for years. Even today you can look in your local newspaper and see organizations throwing a "Tom Sawyer Party" for people to come help them paint something.

Negative stories (such as how boring it is to paint) cast their spell and, unless we see that clearly, we can get bound up in them, not knowing the power we have to change them. Take Burton's decision to tell a new story about his time clock. It isn't painting a fence or punching a time clock that's hard to take.

It's the story about it.

Chapter 13

The Story of Giving and Taking

"If it's not fun, you're not doing it right."

—Fran Tarkenton

A woman I will call Evelyn called me to say that she had just received a $30-million gift for her foundation just north of San Francisco. Even by my standards, this was high. From a single individual? Thirty million dollars? Wow.

"How did it happen?" I asked.

"We just used your system and created the relationship with him," she said. "We shifted our roles the way you say."

"That usually works, but $30 million? Wow."

What did Evelyn mean when she said she "shifted" the roles in the relationship? She meant that she shifted her own role from being a taker to being a giver. And she shifted the donor's role from being a giver to being a taker.

In fundraising, it turns out, when you shift from being a taker to being a giver, you open up the hidden floodgates. Because you can't out-give the Giver, the ultimate Giver that some call by spiritual names and some call "the universe." The more you try, the more you get back. That's a law of the universe, albeit quite hidden.

Quite hidden away! Most people don't know the power of true unconditional giving. They're too busy trying to figure out what they will *get* to stop and listen to the music of the spheres. They spend their lives here on earth trying to calculate their efforts based on what they think the return might be, so they spend their days in hesitation and calculation. They don't end up getting very much. If they would give instead of trying to get, the universe would give back.

Does this sound too mystical to be practical? Well, hang on. It's as real as death and taxes. It brings in real money. In ways that you can statistically measure. It brings in money enough to run an organization or feed a host of families.

A few years back at the University of Arizona, a young assistant track coach named

Mike Bassoff had made quite a reputation for himself recruiting athletes to the U. It didn't hurt that his head coach was Willie Williams, nationally known for his charisma and track-coaching prowess. He was an African-American at a time when many of the top athletes were also African-American, and most head track coaches were not.

Willie Williams was also known to be a fun and funny man. Lighting up a room with his smile and humor and great energy. One day, young Mike Bassoff walked into Coach Williams's office and found him dead. Shot to death. With his own gun, and lying on the floor, an incomprehensibly tragic suicide.

Bassoff was stunned and thrown for a terrible psychological setback himself from this event. He and the coach were close, and Bassoff didn't know what to do next with his career. Suddenly, his taste for coaching had disappeared, and that's when the offer came. Because he'd had success organizing a fundraising "fun run" the year before, Bassoff was offered a position at the university's foundation offices as an assistant fundraiser. His main job would be to keep the annual fun run going, but other duties would be his. And those other year-round fundraising duties he would have to learn from scratch.

"I was a little worried about the whole idea of being a fundraiser because I came from a small blue-collar town in New Jersey and I had no background at cocktail parties or country clubs or golf courses," said Bassoff. "I was worried that I might not fit in or be able to play the game. You know. Rich guys leaning on other rich guys for money at the golf club. I couldn't picture myself in that scene."

Most people would have nurtured the downside of that story. They would have had the story of their modest New Jersey neighborhood up-bringing be the story of their limitation. Mike could have used it to explain away why he never became all that good at fundraising.

But he chose not to do that.

He chose to make that story part of his strength and charm. It was just a choice. It had no independent "truth" to it until Mike started applying the truth. Somehow Mike Bassoff knew deep down something that it took me years to struggle to learn: we *create* truth for our lives by our actions and bold efforts.

Soon he received a major fundraising assign-
ment in addition to the annual fun run. He was
put in charge of raising money for the brand-
new, soon-to-be-built Arizona Cancer Center.
It was then that Mike called me up and asked
me to come help him. I'd never met him. He
had seen and liked a media campaign I'd helped
create for a local political candidate who had
just won an upset election, and he thought I
might help him create some communication
pieces for his fundraising projects.

As I sat in his office, listening to his story about
not liking cocktails and not playing golf and
coming from blue-collar New Jersey and
coaching sports, I wondered how we were ever
going to succeed at raising large amounts of
money for the Cancer Center from wealthy
donors.

Everyone said raising money was hard to do.
That was the story, anyway. You had to trade
favors, schmooze, and cultivate rich people as
you do plants. After awhile, Mike and I had
figured out that this was a very limiting story
holding back the raising of money. The story
was this: it's hard and unpleasant to ask people
for their hard-earned money, but somebody's
got to do it!

Even years later, as consultants going around the country showing various fundraising groups how our "relationshift" system worked, we keep encountering The Story! People doing everything they can to avoid the worst part of fundraising: the terrifying event that they called "The Ask!" People who resent rich people, spending all their office time *getting ready* for their presentations. They call it being prepared. They practice their pitch. Finally off they go, sometimes three of them at a time, to ask for money. When they get to the rich person's home or office, their first thought is, "Boy, can I ever *NOT* relate! I have *no idea* what it is to be rich in this way. I remember asking my dad for money, but this is even scarier."

The problem was right there: boy, can I ever *NOT* relate!

If you can't relate, you can't help someone. And somehow Mike and I knew that to be great at fundraising you had to take the position of helping the donor. Helping the donor realize his or her dream of making a difference in this world.

So the flawed, entrenched, traditional system as we saw it was this: *I can't relate to you, but please give me money.* We found that this is basically how money is raised across the United States of America. Frightened people doing something they hate. You can predict the success rate of just about *anything* that features people doing something they hate. People doing something they fear.

In any walk of life it will fail. Imagine it in a marriage: "I won't learn to relate to you, but let's try to get back together."

People hate to ask other people for money. Can you blame them? Why would that taker's approach be fun for *anyone?*

So Mike and I realized that for us to succeed at raising money we would have to change the system. We'd have to focus on giving instead of getting. Because only that shift would ensure that we were doing something we enjoyed.

That's the key to success right there. It's in the words of the great pro football quarterback Fran Tarkenton, who said, "If it's not fun, you're not doing it right." There was huge wisdom in those words.

But the secret to fun is work. So Mike Bassoff worked hard for his donors. Disproportionately to what they donated. He gave them information about cancer. He had doctors come to their communities and give slide shows about research breakthroughs. He helped relatives in distant states get in to see medical experts for second opinions. He treated donors as though they were gold. He kept at it. He kept outgiving the giver. He kept using the power of his well-kept secret. He knew there was work involved when it comes to fun.

If I sat you down at the piano and asked you to "have fun" for the next hour, the amount of fun you could have at that piano would depend on the amount of work you'd put in to playing it over the years, learning to play, practicing, and performing. The connection between work and fun is always hidden away by advertisers and other peddlers of instant pleasure. In some respects, it has never been revealed before. Or at least it feels that way. It sure seems as though we put comfort and instant pleasure ahead of work. Sometimes we are even *offended* by the idea of work. When a politician suggests an alternative to a handout, perhaps an incentive tied to real work, the prevailing media and political groups call that demeaning and offensive. How dare you suggest work? Many parents today actually protest the fact that their kids are getting homework. This attitude has put American children at a severe disadvantage. Because other cultures still teach the value of work and *their* kids will get all the challenging, knowledge-based jobs in the future. Our kids will be mopping up the fast food restaurant after closing with their MP3 players in their ears while the restaurant owners are speaking Chinese on their cell phones to loved ones back home. And it's good that this will happen. Because it will wake everyone up to the beauty of real work. It will wake the world up to the fun.

When he was a track coach, Mike Bassoff enjoyed recruiting. He was excellent at it. He outperformed most other college track coaches because of the relationships he created with the athletes' families. It was the work he put in learning to relate and connect. He would give a lot of his time and attention to the families of the athletes. He would be the giver in the relationship, not the taker.

We realized that, for our fundraising projects to succeed, we would want to do the same thing. And for that, we had to change the story of fundraising itself from a story of taking to a story of giving. And once we did, it worked miracles. We wrote a book together about the successes we had *(Relationshift).* Because once we changed the story, we changed the results.

It was as if a secret key went into a secret lock and the money flowed in. You can't out-give the universe! The more you give, the more it gives back. We changed the story of fundraising from taking to giving.

Chapter 14

Your Choice: Pleasure or Happiness?

"The last time I saw Elvis he was shooting at a color TV, the phones were ringing in the pink motel and the rest is history."

—Neil Young

I have a friend who planned his life carefully. He bought the story early that succeeding financially and saving your money would allow you to have an early retirement! And, of course, someone retiring early would be awfully lucky, right?

Just as that lucky guy we heard about growing up who "never had to work a day in his life." That was considered the ultimate in good fortune. Whenever someone came upon great financial windfall, people would say, enviously and admiringly, "He'll never have to work again!" How great that sounded.

Except that my friend is miserable.

I won't use his real name here, I'll just call him Early Win. Early wanders about his house, as does Hugh Hefner, in pajamas and slippers. Isn't he in heaven? No, he's miserable.

He has a nagging feeling he's not ... something ... he's not something, but what? What is it? Not producing? Not creating? Not contributing? Not important? He can't put his finger on it. So he sets up lots of social encounters with others who also have nothing to do, and together they talk and talk and tell stories and get their excitement level very high while brandy is socked away, and soon the room is full of great cheer and laughter as in an F. Scott Fitzgerald scene. But what happens the next morning? Early is in his slippers, sipping coffee, reading a huge edition of the newspaper, thinking, "I'm reading, and that's got to be a good thing, right?" But he doesn't feel so good.

Early had always pictured his retirement, and the picture was always based on the concept of pleasure. What gave Early Win pleasure? Travel! And cocktail parties. And the luxury to be able to read late into the morning, then go out on a veranda and read in the afternoon. Then meet with people for cocktails. What pleasure. How luxurious!

But what Early hadn't factored in was how relative everything in life turned out to be. His "pleasure" in the past was largely due to the fact that he had just finished a brutal month of hard work, late hours, difficult projects completed, and exhausting efforts.

Then the pleasures were taken with an underlying sense of satisfaction. "I've worked so hard," thought Early. "I deserve this win," thought Early Win.

What Early had never worked out in his mind was the difference between pleasure and happiness. To him, they were pretty much the same. When I tried to tell him my theory of how different they were, he said I was "splitting hairs."

"Semantics!" he used to say to me whenever I tried to lure him into a conversation about the difference. But for me, it was such a hard-won distinction, I wanted to talk about it. I'd paid a big price to learn about it. I'd gotten it so wrong it had almost killed me.

Pleasure was the ego seeking instant gratification. Pleasure was the second piece of chocolate cake. Happiness, on the other hand, was walking down the lane 2 pounds lighter and feeling more energy because of the new program of exercise and healthy food. That was happiness. Pleasure was the extra cake being chewed up in the mouth. That was pleasure. Happiness was often the feeling of being lighter and more in control of your life force.

Whereas pleasure did not last. And pleasure was worse than that. Not only did pleasure not last, it did something even more upsetting. It turned itself around. It turned itself inside out, like one of those reversible hand puppets that are angels on the one side and devils on the other. Because what is happening to me now? I am only an hour past the eating of the cake, and I am feeling a little sick! A little bloated! Where's the pleasure? It was the best devil's food cake ever! Why can't I still enjoy it? What kind of a cruel joke does pleasure play on me? Not only am I not feeling pleasant about having eaten the cake, I am feeling downright bad about it. I am angry with myself. I am disgusted. So I stand up, in my slippers, and adjust my robe and go to the veranda to read the paper. I will make myself smarter and more knowledgeable. I'll add knowledge to my life. It needs *something* added to it.

But soon I find that I've just spent the past half hour reading about a celebrity divorce!

Why do I waste my time this way? Movie stars, American and utterly without any acting talent, but so cute and over-publicized our nation is following their every move off camera. And we feel that we know them now. So it's fascinating to see that they are getting divorced and she has three children, one from a previous marriage to a famous director, and two adopted with the current, soon-to-be ex-husband, little kids from abroad. Toys, really. I think in my delicious condescending way, these people just collect children as toys. Little human playthings. Look at the pictures. They have these little tykes in their arms, kids from all nations, kids of all colors, toys they are, soon to be discarded, like stuffed animals, and left with nannies. No, wait, what's this story? Oh, he's in *love,* now, with the nanny! And they are going to adopt! He's off to Katmandu to check out new toy babies. On their SUV there is a sticker that says "He Who Dies With The Most Toys Wins!"

So now a half hour has gone by, because one story leads to another, and now I'm on the sports page, and soon the day feels lost. Lost!

And this is just how Early Win feels so often. What is this early retirement all about? Why don't they ever tell you what a nightmare it can be? *How hypocritical of the human race to no longer care for me now that I'm retired.*

Early Win calls upstairs to his wife, who is pounding away on some exercise machine trying to make sense of her own retirement by working her body. Brutally, rigorously, avidly sweating it all out. The body must be the answer to all this nothingness. Taking care of the body. And family. Early Win calls up to her. Early thinks he has it figured out.

"Family!" he yells up the winding staircase. "It's all about family!"

"What is?" she calls down between huffing and puffing on the exerciser.

"Life!" shouts Early Win.

And his wife just shakes her head, wishing Early would pick up some kind of hobby that occupied him more than just reading and following sports and having a cocktail party or two.

Early shouts again, "It's family, isn't it?"

And Early doesn't wait for her reply, but instead goes to the phone in the sunroom and picks it up and starts dialing his daughter's number, and he's about halfway through her number when he realizes that she's at work. In her part of the world it's work time and she's working in her accounting firm. Wow, he thinks. She loves numbers, she always loved numbers and music and he was happy to tell her, to educate her, really, about how they were connected. Almost the same thing. The notes on the scale, the matching harmonies, the mathematics of music! In fact, Early has thought of writing a book called *The Mathematics of Music.*

"But who would read it?" he shouts up the staircase to no response.

So this guy I'm calling Early is in torment rather than in retirement. Oh, it's not the story he tells. His story is that he is in heaven, doing everything he always wanted to do. Dabbling in this and that.

But he's been let down by pleasure. That's his anger. He's found out that you can't get to happiness by adding more pleasure. It had seemed that you could. It had seemed that you ought to be able to get to happiness by increasing the amount of pleasure in your life, but it never happened. In fact, it's never happened for anyone.

Sometimes I ride along in my car and I play some of my favorite Elvis Presley songs, and my kids, my wife, and my family always ask, "Is that young Elvis or old Elvis?" They want to know. Because young Elvis was so good. The range on that voice! Amazing. And the power and freedom of expression was so joyful. The "old" Elvis (although not all that old in calendar years) sounded pretty bad. And felt pretty bad. It was sad to realize how pleasure had taken him down so low. His last song recorded was even called "Way Down."

When you glance, even just casually, at the life of Elvis Presley, you can see the happiness that was so joyfully there when he was working so hard in his younger years making all those great records, doing take after take after take. Stories were circulating about him taking 10, 20—no 30—takes to get "Hound Dog" just right, so that it truly rocked through and through up to the last note. To create that wired, spent, thrilled-out sound, that rasping psyched voice carrying the wild energy of the new rock-and-roll era all in one fearless heart. The *work* that took was exhilarating! But the work was so worth it. You saw young Elvis on TV performing and the joy in his body and smile and leer. In his whole unfettered, unbound persona. That was one amped-up and happy wild male.

Then what happened? You can hear his decline in the music itself. You can hear his voice getting thicker and less inspired with each passing year. What was going on? You could see his movies getting worse and worse. And look at the man they call the King! He's fat! Wow, he's really getting chubby. What's going on? And later stories came out about his pleasure, his adding pleasure onto pleasure. Deep-fried peanut butter and banana sandwiches cooked up again and again and again by a private cook at Graceland. All the sumptuous, nonstop, at-his-fingertips eating, and the drugs. The drugs they found in his body were startling. Even to those of us who had taken a drug or two in the Flower Power era, this list of drugs was staggering. How could one simple 260-pound being contain so many drugs? These drugs were found in his body at the autopsy: Morphine, Quaaludes, Valium, Diazepam, Placidyl, Amytal, Nembutal, Carbrital, Demerol, Sinutab, Elavil, Avental, and Valmid.

So much pleasure, so little time.

Dead at 42.

Pleasure is not happiness. Though we spread the story that it is.

"We're really looking forward to our vacation," my friend Yvonne told me a few months ago. "It's going to be so great. Out on the islands, with no worries, great food, and cheap paperback novels. Wow. We've been saving up for this for a long time. I am so glad that Jeffrey can finally get away from his work to enjoy this. I'm worried about him. I'm afraid he might have a heart attack, given his hours and stress. This will be great for him."

A month later I asked how the islands vacation went, and Yvonne didn't want to talk about it. She and Jeffrey were in counseling now, and the real trouble started on that vacation.

"Some of the things we said to each other were just so mean," she told me. "We had to check it out. We had to find out if we even liked each other."

They thought they could overwhelm their lack of happiness with some South Sea Island *pleasure.* But they are two entirely different things. They just didn't know that.

I remember my father once telling me that he and my mother were happiest when I was very little.

"We both worked so hard back then, it's ironic that those were the happy times," he said, not understanding. "Then, after a week at work, we spent the weekend working on our little house and yard together. We worked on it Saturday and Sunday. I couldn't afford much, so it was a big deal to get a case of beer and have some neighbors come over in the evening and just sit out in the backyard and look at the sky and talk about the gardening and fix-up things we were working on."

Later in the marriage, more pleasure got factored in, and, as is always the case, more happiness got factored out. Out with the work, out with the happiness. My mother took to the world of pharmaceuticals to fill the void, the deep hole of emptiness that too much pleasure brings, and my dad filled it up with more business trips than he needed to make, flying his own plane, more and more drinking, and you already know this story.

If people could just appreciate the distinction between happiness and pleasure, they would avoid so much pain. Pleasure brings pain, and happiness brings deeper happiness. Is that so hard for everybody to figure out? (I guess so! Although it only took *me* 40 years.)

So let's look at the story that says early retirement is automatically always a good thing that everyone ought to dream about. It certainly wasn't for my friend Early Win.

But can it be? I believe it can if one notices the connection between good, challenging work and happiness. I cited someone the opposite of Early Win earlier: Terry Hill. My co-author of the book *Two Guys Read Moby-Dick.* Terry grasped quickly that if he was going to make his own early retirement work, he would have to work. So he set about with some rigorous writing disciplines for himself. (For it was not lightheartedly that the great author Anthony Burgess once said, "Writing a book is the hardest work a human can do.")

Terry wrote a mystery novel, set in the world of advertising, his former life. Terry also took up art. He worked hard at that, too. Even had a showing in New York of his art. Early in his retirement he intuited that pleasure could take him down. At any moment.

But he is rare compared to most of us. We just don't understand this. We try to *avoid* work! We try to get out of it! We even help our kids out so they don't "have to" work. We leave huge sums of money to our children. Then we use the term *spoiled* when referring to them. Interesting phrase, isn't it, when applied to humans? Spoiled.

How is food spoiled? By leaving it out in some warm, cushy environment where it doesn't have to work against the cold to stay fresh. *Where it doesn't have to work to stay fresh.*

Jean Paul Sartre said that the greatest gift a father could give his child would be to die by the time the child is 7 years old. That was a startling statement, but you see his point. That child, provided the first seven years were well-attended by the father, would now have to work. Really work.

So I want to remind myself daily that I want to work to stay fresh. And to do so, I must constantly change the story in my head about early retirement. If I do "retire" I want to step up the work, not wind it down. No one wants another Elvis around the house.

Chapter 15

Do You Love Him to Death?

"Once you realize that the road is the goal
and that you are always on the road,
not to reach a goal,
but to enjoy its beauty and its wisdom,
life ceases to be a task and becomes natural
and simple,
in itself an ecstasy."

—Sri Nisargadatta Maharaj

What road will you take? Your journey on that road is more important and more vital than your story, because your journey is full of fun and travel and action and footwork. Whereas your story is full of opinions and hot air and the mirages called "arriving" and "making it."

Let others learn of your journey and tell your story for you. The story of Lazarus was told by people who witnessed it, not by the person who performed the healing. Don't worry about your story. Live so enthusiastically that others follow you around taking notes, writing your story for you. Let them try to keep up with you.

When you have your life be more about your journey than your story, you'll see what happens. What will happen? You might reinvent yourself! Which is to say, you might abandon old stories.

I received an e-mail on my computer the morning I sat down to write this chapter. I decided to open it and read it, and then go back to writing this chapter. Two unrelated things. So I thought, until I read the e-mail:

Dear Mr. Chandler:

My friend recommended your book about reinvention to me and, although I felt that no amount of anything could save me from myself (I am a addict of 20-plus years who has been in and out of recovery, dysfunctional relationships, 12-step programs, etc.), I decided that I couldn't get more screwed up than I possibly am, so I went out and bought it a month ago. At that point I had been clean 37 days from a debilitating cocaine habit that has taken me in and out of recovery for the past 15 years.

I am a 40-year-old adult who desperately needs to grow up, a true victim. My mother always used to say to me, "Peter, there is no room for a child in an adult world." I blamed everyone around me for my crappy existence, my drug addiction, etc. Why does everything "happen" to me? I used to ponder this question often through chemistry. I hated myself, I'm good for nothing, I suck, etc. Why even bother? All the negative tapes have been rolling through my head for years. I have been in counselling, 12-step fellowships, taken courses in psychology and anything else short of ending it to figure out what is wrong with me, and then I started reading this frightening book of yours....

Your book lit the fire in my soul and under my ass! It really makes sense to me. I feel as I am reading each chapter that you are giving me directions, a blueprint on how to live in this world. This is something I was never taught growing up. I am completely clueless. I am living on disability because being a victim and blaming everyone for being an insensitive ***** (pick a four letter word ... lol) and found every excuse known to man not to have an adult job. Anyway, the owner/victim thing rang clear.

At that moment I decided to become an **OWNER.** I am sick and tired of being a victim.

That very first week I decided to think of a career I would enjoy. I love animals and began to research dog grooming. What would an owner like myself do? This owner, ME! would go interview a variety of people working in different shops as well as owners to find out about the business, which I did. I then convinced the owner of a pet shop to take me on as an apprentice for the month of December. He recommended a school called The Nash Academy of the Grooming Arts for dog grooming, where a state-funded program is going to pay for most of my training! I only have to come up with a relatively small amount! That is what your book has taught me. Follow my dreams. I always had excuses. I thought like a victim and "sentenced myself" out of hopes, dreams, and life. I feel so good to be in the land of the living for once in my life! Yeah! I was spewing over your book to a friend of mine and she just didn't get it. She said, "You read one self help book, you read them all." I thought to myself that she just didn't get it. Victim-thinking for sure!

Have a happy and healthy New Year to you and yours!

Peter M. in Oregon

Peter has a journey going on! And it is obvious that his new story is trying to keep up with his journey. Look how exciting Peter's new journey is. It's so exciting, his old story is now just kind of a dark and flimsy memory to him. It was serious and grave before. It felt all so true before. Being an addict and an immature boy-child unable to fit into a grown-up world. What a story that was. Can you see how his mother got it started? Let's read this e-mail again! You can see the whole of human civilization contained in this letter that arrived from Peter that morning. The very morning I sat down on my own journey to write a chapter to you! Now I'll take whatever side road looks good. Let's cut through the forest!

And let's cut through the nonsense in Peter's life. It is nonsense that Peter is uniquely un-suited for adult life. If he is, we all are. We all have to fake the adult part as we suppress the childlike joy and energy. How ironic that what thrilled our parents the most about us—our first words, our first steps walking—soon became their greatestest source of irritation.

At first it was, "Oh boy, he said something! Wow! Did you hear him? He said 'Da,' or maybe, 'Dad!' Yes, I think I heard 'Dad!'"

Break out the wine. Baby's first words!

Then the next big moment happens when baby walks! Wow! Look at him walk. Everybody cheers as he stagger-steps across the room from Mom's arms to Dad's. Wow. Let's celebrate.

But it's not very long before this joyful verbal and physical self-expression starts to get annoying. I mean, don't get carried away, kid. Soon you hear this: "Quiet! Quiet! No talking!" What? I thought you were celebrating the fact that I could speak. Soon it's also this: "Hey sit, sit, sit! Sit DOWN! Please, just stay STILL! Find a chair, Peter, and sit DOWN!"

Wait a second. I thought you were once weeping for joy at my ability to walk across the room, and now it's a problem?

Yes, it's a problem. If you want to make it in this civilization, you will learn to repress your enthusiasm for life and serve others' needs, not your own. You will anticipate what pleases other people and act accordingly. You will spend your whole life trying (in vain, it will turn out) to live up to other people's expectations of you.

Or you will develop a cocaine habit. A way of going in. A way back to your essence: pure energy and creativity. Except that it will backfire. The energy surge won't last. Satan will be laughing with delight because you'll soon have to use the drug just to feel normal and average! You had to borrow or steal money to score a drug that, after you take it, has the effect on you of lifting you up—feelings-wise—to an average person's bad day! It is not real! Drugs and alcohol were the ultimate in betrayal. They actually robbed you of your essence. They borrowed energy from your future and delivered it in a big, fake jolt into the present moment. But unless you died, you eventually had to visit that future of yours, and those of us who have been there will tell you that the down is not worth the up. This drug is *not* your friend, although the first times you got high you might have thought it was the greatest friend you ever knew. (Elvis, do you have anything to say here? Speak up if you do.)

One of the best things that Peter can realize is that there is a part of him that doesn't want to be a grown-up, and that's the best part of him, not the worst. It was no fluke that the whole world was mesmerized by the story of Peter Pan, the boy who refused to grow up. What Peter showed us was that when you are a child, you can fly.

So the Peter in the e-mail finally got that he was being a victim of circumstance and other people (his story), and not an owner of the spirit and his own unlimited opportunity. By reinventing himself through the book, he saw how his victim story was all made up anyway, so why not make up a new one? Why not make up a story that says I am recovered from that and creating a new life for myself? It might be more useful.

And then, as life becomes a journey, what Peter wants to watch out for is making any new story too permanent. Because if you do, Peter, you could get stuck again. Whereas, if you stay on the journey and never arrive, it just gets better. Don't try to "arrive" or "make it," because that's a trap similar to a drug. That won't serve you, because you'll shut yourself off from all that's possible beyond the new story. Your daily waking up to the journey will save you from that. Keep waking up. Keep going. Beyond the book. Beyond the 12 steps (as transformative and beautifully powerful as they are), and into the glorious, unfolding infinite.

Peter will help a lot of people, and if he stays on his journey, because of how talented he is at expressing his feelings of recovery, people will love him.

I almost said, "People will love him to death." Curious phrase. When people say, "I love him to death," as so many people say now, what do they mean? Do they wish the person dead? Hardly. It means the opposite, doesn't it? Subconsciously, I believe it means "I love him to the death of his story." In other words, I love him, the real him, the essence and spirit down deep beyond his story of himself or other people's story about him, to the death of those stories. That's how deep my love goes, to the place where there is no more story, just him, just his essence, just his very being.

Chapter 16

Stories We Tell to Please Others

"The music business is a cruel and shallow money trench. A long plastic hallway where pimps and thieves run free and good men die like dogs. There is also a negative side."

—Hunter S. Thompson

I'll never forget all the trips and phone calls I made with my great friend and songwriting partner Fred Knipe while he and I were in the music business. We went to the music capitals of the world—Nashville, New York, and Los Angeles—pitching our songs. We so wanted to please producers and publishers that we were willing to be humiliated over and over. It was part of the quest.

One time we won an opportunity to spend time in Los Angeles with legendary music executive Kip Cohen of A&M Records. We were so very excited that we brought into his office demos of our songs—demos that were variously performed by a jazz fusion band, a punk rock group, and songs by a female country-pop artist, all of which we played for the famous Mr. Cohen himself. One song after another. Boy, did those songs of ours sound great on his huge speaker system in his office! Mr. Cohen sat back in his chair and listened carefully, as we tried to read his face. Is he loving our stuff? Is this the break we've waited for? Maybe we've made it. Maybe we have arrived.

After the last song finished playing, Mr. Cohen turned in his chair and said, "You know, fellas, I think I want to tell you something. I think I should. Here it is: when my wife gets sick, I don't like it."

I snuck a glance at Fred to see if he was understanding Mr. Cohen any better than I was at this point, but Fred was just frozen, staring at the top executive, waiting for him to continue, so I decided to do the same.

Then Kip Cohen said, "It doesn't make sense. It's not rational, I know. It's not even fair of me to feel that way about my wife. I love her and she's sick and I'm annoyed at her for being sick, and that doesn't make any sense does it? I mean, it's not her fault."

Fred and I both half-smiled and nodded, and then shook our heads. We didn't know what to say or do. No, it's not her fault, but yes, it is understandable, sir, whatever you want us to think right here, sir, whatever will help us get one or two of these songs picked up by your record label, sir. Our basic position is: whatever!

Cohen continued, "So, in the same way, I shouldn't be as annoyed with you two as I am right now. I know I shouldn't, but I am. I mean, who do you think you *are* playing all these different kinds of songs for me? You know who you remind me of?"

"No, sir. We don't." (Or, at least we can't think, right now, of who we would remind you of.)

"You remind me of a whore! A prostitute! A whore who says I'll perform this act for so much, or I can do that sex act for you and it will cost you that, or I can do this for you. I can do Around the World if you like! Anything!"

Around the World? We said nothing. Both of us were nodding slightly, now. Nodding to show him that we now understood who we reminded him of.

"So do you see what I mean, guys?" Mr. Cohen said. "I know you're fine young men, and I like you. I really do. And even these songs—they're not all that bad, do you know what I mean? I'm just saying that your approach, offering this and that and all kinds of totally unrelated things to me, it's like what that prostitute would do. That's all I'm saying."

"Sure, of course," Fred said as he and I stood to leave. We shook hands with Mr. Cohen and left his office in silence.

As we drove away, I asked Fred, "So his point is we are prostitutes for wanting to sell our songs?"

Fred said, "No. His point was in the variety. He was telling us he would have preferred one song. One great song that we were enthusiastic about."

After we were back home and the weeks passed, we decided to take the Kip Cohen wisdom to heart. Cohen was actually right. His wisdom was reinforced during subsequent song pitches we made. "One song" is what the best producers told us they were looking for. So now, when we called record producers, we said we had one killer song. The theory was, they'll play it and, even if it misses, it will make an impression. If the impression is good, we will get another chance.

Fred had helped me turn this incident around in my mind. Because, emotionally, the incident was pure humiliation. "What an ***hole!" was my first measured internal response. I was hurt and stung by the famous Mr. Cohen. But Fred showed me the wisdom in not being stuck in that bad story about what had happened on our visit. He showed me how it would benefit us as songwriters not to offer "Around the World" anymore. It was too needy.

In later years I would use a version of this hard-earned wisdom in training salespeople not to be needy. Needy is creepy. It creeps people out, to put it in a more contemporary vernacular.

We also learned this: Focus your best effort into the song, not just into what you say about the song. (Or who you see about the song.) The songs Fred and I had the most success with were songs we didn't pitch at all. They were songs that seemed to pitch themselves whenever we sent them out. The selling was already inside the songs.

Some of my clients today are also speakers and authors. Sometimes they write a book quickly and then want to talk to me about marketing their book. They want to know all the latest Internet schemes and scams for promoting their book. They are really ready to make an effort, they tell me. This book "means a lot" to them and they want to "go all out" to promote it.

Sometimes it crosses my mind: Should I be honest right away? Should I say what I think immediately? Or later? The "promotion effort" should go into the book itself. The marketing should go into the product itself, not the marketplace.

The best and best-selling books market them-selves. Because people read them and then they tell their friends about them, and then they buy copies for their family members, and it spreads around. Especially today, now that the world has been flattened by the Internet. When something is fun to read, the world knows about it by tomorrow night.

In the not-so-distant past, the world still had many mountainous hierarchies. To get your book "out there" you had to romance agents and publishers and bookstore managers and a whole piled-up tower of petty but powerful people. Today, it's just write a great book and BOOM! The blogs and e-mail communications go whipping electronically around the world in a heartbeat. You can't stop something interesting from getting around. It tells its own story.

So the point is to focus right now in this creative moment. This book, this speech, this conversation—whatever "this" is for you. The effect of leveraging the present moment is where all the power is. I like to call this the "Lazarus Effect." It's inspired by the story of Jesus raising Lazarus from the dead. (You can tell that I like this story by how often I mention it.)

The Lazarus Effect is a powerful effect that can apply to any profession. Let's say you are a consultant or a sales professional and you want more business. To utilize the Lazarus Effect, you wake up and enter your day committed. Committed! You are committed to having each conversation you are in produce a miracle. You bring total focus to each exchange with another person. You bring total focus to each task before you. You are focused on what the conversation can produce for the other person. If you are taking an hour to write a portion of a new proposal, you bring total focus to that.

If you attack, full-out, each task in front of you that way, you won't have to promote yourself, others will. They'll do it for free. You won't have to worry about your life "turning out" or how to increase the hype for yourself. You won't have to go see Mr. Cohen with your tail tucked between your legs, because the power will already have been in the songs themselves. He will have already heard of you.

The best example of this process at work is the story of Lazarus. By giving all his attention to Lazarus (remember: *all* his attention—he wasn't glancing around wondering how he was coming across, or who was there to be impressed), Jesus created a miracle and raised that poor deceased person from the dead! Jesus didn't need to hand out brochures to promote himself after that. He didn't have to remember to make a video of his encounter with Lazarus to stream on his Website for promotional value. The word got out by itself. They are still talking about it today! More than 2,000 years later, the story still goes around and around. That's the power of full attention.

People write their books quickly and don't give full attention to them. Then they spend hours trying to promote and sell their hastily written books. (And when I say "books," substitute in whatever you do.)

"How do I promote my book?" a client named Dillon asked me.

"Go write it again," I said.

"How do you mean?"

"Go through your book, sentence by sentence, and write each sentence over again."

"You must be kidding."

"I will tell you the quote from Robert Frost that I have up in my office to remind me to go back and do all my writing over again, once more with feeling."

"What is the quote?"

"Frost said, 'No tears in the writer, no tears in the reader.'"

"I have to cry?"

"It would help."

"How?"

"You have put your head into your book, but not your heart. You have not only put your head in it, but you have put your fast-forward, greed-head into it. You are racing forward to the future sales of the book with no care for the poor reader. There is no gift for the reader if you do this so fast, as part of your rush-rush life of multitasking and enforced busy-ness and a longing to live in your own future."

Dillon thought for a moment and asked me, "Write the whole thing over?"

"At least once," I said.

"Do you have any idea how *hard* that would be?"

"I do."

Dillon did, too. Or at least he could imagine it. So he didn't write it over, he jumped right into the promo phase and devoted hours and hours promoting. He never sought my advice again, and the last I heard he was spending huge amounts of time in bookstores at book signings that sometimes attracted as many as seven buyers. At this rate he would have to live 2,000 years to have his book crack the Amazon Top 100. But he was healthy, so you never know.

I've been at those book signings where sometimes long lines of three or four people would come to the bookstore to have you sign your book. A whole afternoon at a bookstore and four people bought books to be signed. All this frantic effort to polish and buff up the *story of the book*—and, therefore, the story of you—and no effort going into the book itself.

Dillon may never learn. But it's true. If you will stay focused on the miracle you can produce in this one encounter in front of you right now—in Dillon's case the encounter between him and his reader—all your "promo" will be handled in the moment. It shows up in the future, but it's handled in the moment. We have *no idea* how much we create in each present moment. Because we don't see it with our instant-gratification eyes, we don't think anything is happening.

It's happening.

I often use the Lazarus Effect to snap me out of some sleepwalking I'm doing through my daily existence. I might be talking to someone during a break at one of my seminars and catch my fatigued mind drifting as I worry that this person is not "important enough" to give my full attention to. Forgetting as I am that all people are important and all people are connected, and now is the moment, and only now, to connect. I'm forgetting until I think of Lazarus. Lazarus was not a very important person. He was a kind of "unimportant" person back then, and then you add in the fact that he was dead, and in Lazurus you don't have, really, the guy in your address book that you've highlighted with a yellow marker.

But it's our job to wake up and connect and see the blessedness and divinity in every single person. That's our only job. Because the most unimportant person always turns out to be the most important. And the most "important" person turns out to be pathetically petty just like you and me. Therefore, we're doing our best work when we treat each person as if he or she is gold.

It's even our job, sometimes, to bring people back from the dead. Sometimes we can do it with a touch of praise or a dash of humor, but it is why we are here on this planet. We are all here to bring each other back.

Chapter 17

Where Do We Get Our Willpower?

"The past beats inside me like a second heart."

—John Banville

Many sundowns ago I was visiting my mentor, the supercoach Steve Hardison, and I was asking him about discipline. I was concerned that I might not have any.

He began answering me by talking about what happens when he goes out for a run. How out on the run, many times his body wants to quit, and how he manages not to quit.

I got excited by this example because it sounded as if it was just what I needed to learn about. A way to find whatever controls the "quit switch" inside of me.

I said to him, "That thing that switches 'Quit' into 'Don't Quit' is where I need to go."

I knew that will and discipline were potential missing pieces in my daily life. I wanted his help with correcting that. Everything in my life seemed fine but that. I had a wonderful wife, a wonderful profession, my skills were way up to speed, and everything seemed fully developed for difference-making and happiness but that one thing. Internal discipline.

I knew from all the therapy and spiritual work I had done that when something comes up missing in one's operating system there is usually a deep childhood wound. Everyone, no matter how well-raised, has them. And whatever my own childhood wound was, it was causing that thing they call discipline to be hidden away.

I said to Steve Hardison, "What you use as 'will,' when you run, or when you do anything, I think I have simply surrendered. Or maybe I've just turned it over to other people."

He asked what I meant by that.

"Well, I think I survive because of the will of others. I do everything based on what I think others want. Not on what I want."

We could see that that was a very powerless position for me to take. Because it meant that everything was done in anticipation of other people's judgment of it. And that's an orientation to life that's outside-in. It builds extra steps and levels into the process of action. It focuses on the external part of life—other people and circumstances. And it ignores the true source of power. No wonder my recurring feeling was often powerlessness. It was as if there was a hole in me that ought to be filled with something powerful, but remained empty since childhood.

"What do you want?" Steve asked me.

"Well ... I'm not sure. But when there is a certain something that right now needs to be done, I want my lifeforce to rush up into that hole so I have *will* to do it!"

It was dawning on me that only external fearful events forced my will to show up. As a system, it did work. It had worked for me for years. And I kept my life evolving upward by choosing better and better people to respond to. (And to be afraid of.) And when I put something into a category called *survival,* it got done. But it was all about giving to, pleasing, and manipulating the *outside* world.

And, therefore, when that outside world looked as though it was going to kill me, I could find the will. What did that mean about me? Did it mean that my ego didn't let me have the will unless the ego (personality, the story of me) looked as if it was about to be *crushed* by something?

During my shameful and youthful drug days, amphetamines were always appealing because they were a temporary cure for this. I learned in college that, on speed, you can do just about anything. Even pass courses. Of course, then you crash and get sick and die, so it isn't the answer. (Nor do you remember anything about the courses.) Drugs rob from the future to deliver a false rush to the present. Not a good investment.

So given that I've recovered from all that madness, how do I now change all this? Poet W.H. Auden once said, "We would rather be ruined than change," and that's how desperately we cling to these stories such as "I have no will!" It seems that we *know* they are true. We never even question them. Even if we come to ruin. Our story is still there to explain and excuse the ruin. I didn't succeed because I just couldn't.

I believe that, in childhood, somewhere I had shut down and played dead in response to something. Somehow I programmed in "I CAN'T" for survival. (If you can't, who can blame you if you don't? All childhood survival is the survival of potential humiliation.) That's why I now needed to develop a fresh will I could call on, a will not hidden away by my memories.

My consultant Steve and I worked on that hole in me. And he is a great coach. Soon we could actually see that the hole in me was designed to contain my will but did not. And the more we relaxed into allowing that hole to just be, the more it began to fill with light and warmth. I began to see that "will" was there for me to use all along. It was always down there next to the hole, waiting to be invited in, living at the level of choice. So all I'd had to do was choose it! Or not. It was so simple, but because it was so simple, I had missed it all my life.

Steve asked me if I was willing to do something physical to anchor my enlightenment. He asked if I had ever been thrown into a pool during one of the wild parties of my youth.

"Yes, I have," I said.

"But were you sober?"

"Probably not."

"Are you willing to come outside to the pool?"

"Sure," I said.

And it wasn't long before I was standing next to a very cold pool at Steve's house with him. He stated to me again that what was missing in me was a certainty, deep down, that I had the will and power to do anything I chose to do.

"You have inner programming that says *'I can't,'*" said Steve. "In the face of any challenge, those words come up from that hole in you. We are going to replace them, by choice, with the words *I can.* Because you know you really can."

He asked me to remove my wallet and items from my pockets and take my shoes off. And with that, he grabbed me, put me up on his shoulders, and got ready to launch me deep into the water. I stopped him. I asked if we shouldn't go into this water in stages. Maybe go down the steps in the shallow end. So it wouldn't be such a shock. As soon as I said it,

I realized what I was doing. There it was! The *I can't* had just spoken. Steve saw it, too.

"No," he said. "You can do this."

I nodded to him, showing him that I had chosen to do this. I had chosen *I can.*

He tossed me into the deep end. Then he jumped in after! It was cold. Very cold. And it was liberating.

From that moment on I felt different. I felt a connection to choice I'd never felt before. And just for practice, I kept saying the words *I can,* filling the hole again and again.

Then, on a morning three days after that visit with Steve, I decided to observe this thing—this power of *I can*—in action. I had about 30 heavy bags of branches that I had told myself (and others) that I would take out from the far back of the backyard to the front curb. Big, floppy, unwieldy, heavy, nasty, breaking-apart, filthy bags with sharp, brittle, thorny sticks sticking out in the Arizona heat. So when I started to do this task, I observed myself, and I witnessed my thoughts and feelings, as if I were watching someone else in a movie. I saw myself deciding to just do a few bags for now. Stages. They were heavy and hard to carry to the front curb from the backyard, so I decided I would do just a few. So I took two bags, then four bags, out. Then I decided to notice what my mind and body were saying, and they were saying to me, "That's enough for now." And I immediately thought of Steve Hardison saying, "The body wants to quit, about 10 times during the run. It wants to quit! But I don't quit." So I just thought, "Oh look, my body wants to quit. My body wants to quit now, and my feelings agree." But there is something observing this phenomenon. Who's watching? And what if whoever is watching just says, "Okay, you guys want to quit, but keep going anyway. Just go anyway. You can."

So I just said that to myself and I kept going. I went back for another bag, and then another. Soon I felt like a happy animal, divorced from human emotion. Then I caught the body and mind (and feelings) wanting to quit again, and I just said, "Oh look! The body-mind wants to quit again, but that's okay, just keep going."

Pretty soon the wanting-to-quit thought-feelings faded away completely. They were similar to a kid pouting and going home with his ball. A kid saying, "If no one's going to take me seriously, I'm just going home." And the job got done.

When it was done, I stood back and admired an enormous pile of heavy, chock-full yard bags piled up in a neat order at the front curb for the trash pick-up. Amazing.

You might not have any way of relating to what I just described. Because our holes are all different. Some people have easy access to the "I can" switch that controls their will and power. Especially for something as simple as yard work. Some have their holes where love or listening or decision-making want to be. But it's all the same void. It's all an absence of the awareness of the power of choice inside of us. A surrender of this power to other people and circumstance, so that life becomes outside-in, annoying and frightening.

So the yard bags might look to some people to be nothing! No breakthrough at all. But for me they were something. Because how I usually did these tasks was to base it all on how little I can get away with. The minimum effort. Two bags a day. That's okay isn't it? That's actually not bad, given that *I can't.*

What will others think? What do they expect? Evaluate that and do the minimum. That's the system. And believe me, I have done a lot this way. I have accomplished a great deal. I have written a lot, coached a lot, trained a lot, and had days when I did a lot! People called me "prolific." But there was always a problem with it. I had always done it all based on what was pressing in on me from the outside. When does the publisher need this book? Can I have 30 more days? If you shelve the "will," it goes so deep in you that it comes out perverted on the other side of the universe as "another person." It then commands you posing as "another."

So if the IRS needed a payment, I went into crazy action. If certain vital bills were due, I stepped up the energy. If some family member was hurting or feeling neglected, I was there, making up for lost time. Overcompensating based on what's coming in from the outside world. It's a perversion of the will. A perversion of the beauty of the soul that wants to show up and express itself as pure, joyful action, unattached to outside pressure and other people's stories.

Chapter 18

Success and Failure Slow a Body Down

"There's no success like failure,
and failure's no success at all."

—Bob Dylan

The brilliant and innovative Texas Tech football coach Mike Leach says, "Both failure and success slow players down, unless they *will* themselves not to slow down."

Failure and success are both external stories about neutral events. They are stories that breed the chains that slow you down. (Unless you *will* yourself not to slow down.) The story called failure, once you let yourself get into the story, and roll around in it, can bring you down. You become discouraged. Soon you might even see yourself as a loser.

The story of success can pump you up! But soon you might be gloating and vulnerable. You might become arrogantly ignorant of your need to continuously learn the game, grow the skill, and fire up the will. The story of success allows you to think you have already *arrived* somewhere.

Remember that Elvis had also "arrived." No pop singer had ever been more "successful." His identifying with that story turned him from pure muscle and fire into cold, pale fat, lying dead on the bathroom floor at the age of 42. A story about "making it" did that.

And speaking of making it, F. Scott Fitzgerald was the very picture of a success story in 1920. He had just married the beautiful Zelda, and he had just published *This Side of Paradise.* His was a storybook life and he knew it. At that time he wrote, "Riding in a taxi one afternoon between very tall buildings under a mauve and rosy sky, I began to bawl because I had everything I wanted and I knew I would never be so happy again."

Most success stories end in moments such as this. With the hero riding under a rosy sky of pure illusion. Suddenly sad. Because all good stories come to an end. That's always the problem with stories.

Fitzgerald panicked at his foresight and soon tried to cover the panic with greater and greater pleasures. His life descended into drinking alcohol and writing bad Hollywood screenplays. A wonderful writer wasted his body and his talent and was dead by the age of 44.

I thought of his body and Elvis's body when I got an e-mail from Matt Furey. Matt was a collegiate national wrestling champion (NCAA 2, 1985) and world Kung Fu Shuai-Chiao champion (Beijing, 1997). Matt likes to get right to the point. His e-mail said, "Hi, Steve. The more you conquer your physical body through exercise, the easier it is to conquer anything else in your life."

I looked up from the e-mail from Matt and thought for a minute. Most of my life I had thought that conquering inner demons was a matter of psychological work and spiritual work. Physical exercise? What did that have to do with anything? I looked back down at the e-mail and kept reading.

"There's a reason for this, too," Matt said. "Although we tend to divide everything into the compartments of mind, body—and so on—what IF—and this is a profound question—what IF they are one in the same. I suggest that they are, and I'm not alone in this idea. In fact, it goes back thousands of years. Train the body and you simultaneously train the mind."

Isn't that what happened when I just had the body take the heavy bags out despite what the mind and emotions were saying? Didn't my mind eventually give up, given that the body was already in action? Given that the body was simply going to do it anyway?

The body is a funny thing, isn't it? It is said that, in America, we are obsessed with the body. All the weight-loss books and programs and all the plastic surgery and anorexia among actresses and teenagers. But is this true? It might equally be true that we ignore our bodies. We neglect them by treating them as separate things. We don't have them up there with mind and spirit at all. We fill them up with soda and chips because—relatively speaking—compared to all our other paranoid cares and con-cerns—we don't care at *all* about our bodies as we haul them through airports, wondering if all 300 pounds will fit in the plane seat.

Matt Furey continued by saying, "The purpose of exercise is to increase awareness of your thoughts—and of your feelings—and of how you look, move, stretch, and so on. Those who fol-low what I'm talking about KNOW that you can eliminate and banish fear via exercise, not to mention depression and a host of other negatives."

I got up from reading the e-mail from Matt and took a long walk. On my walk I realized that I can come from that body-honoring place, or I can just react to other people. And it isn't even other people that I'm reacting to. It's their story they have made up about what they think they need from me. As essential people, they don't need anything, but their stories do, because their stories are never enough. What is always needy is the story of who they think they are. All personal stories are deeply needy, even those stories that are boastful! If people were really connected to who they were, they wouldn't need anything. They wouldn't need to boast. There would be no such insecurity.

When I "coach" people, it's my job to connect people to who they really are. To the pure and joyful source of action inside themselves. It's a source of power inside them that gets ignored while they search the eyes of others for their clues as to what their next move should be.

When I took the plunge in the cold water of the pool, I think my own coach and I were trying to dive beneath my story (what my body and mind thought it wanted). To dive beneath everything external and get at that "I *can*" thing and activate it.

As the weeks and months passed, that source of choice got activated sometimes, and then it was gone! I put signs up on my bathroom wall that said "I CAN," but after a while, after feeling beaten down by my stories about travel and deadlines and life, I literally could not remember what those signs meant. I read the two words *(I can!)* on my wall, but now they looked to be a shallow affirmation.

But now, this morning, I wake up really tuned in to what it means. (Thanks, Matt.) It means observe your body. Observe. Observe that the body will want to quit and the mind will want to bail and the system of personality will want to wait till something outside me threatens. There's a perverse and false comfort in that waiting. It feels as though I can hide out and rest in the waiting. Grabbing some relief from the next wave of threats. They will be coming. It's similar to a little boy playing soldiers. Wait! Be quiet. Over that hill! They are coming!

So the childhood message was that you've got to just be ready for them (other people's needs) and respond to them. All these outside people!

Because they are coming at you. Nothing inside you is worth cultivating and nurturing and trusting. Life is about manipulating the Others. It's a horror film. *The Others!*

I saw a comedian in a large hall recently get a huge laugh when he opened his act this way: "Do you know who the people are that I can't stand? Do you know who I really hate? (Long pause.) Others!"

I always wondered what our great American philosopher Ralph Waldo Emerson meant when he said, "It is easy to live for others; everybody does. I call on you to live for yourself."

What? Don't serve others?

But, he did not say "don't serve others." He simply said don't *live for them.* You could probably serve them more, especially if your prosperity isn't where you want it to be. Just don't live for them. Live for yourself! Enter the kingdom within, as Jesus recommended. That alone will serve others more than endlessly trying to please them ever would.

"If you've got the guts to conquer your body, you've got the guts to conquer any area of life you so choose," said Matt Furey. "Conversely, those who do not choose to conquer their body— and ironically, you conquer your body by getting in harmony with it—cannot conquer much else. Yes, there is greatness and power that comes from being able to rule your own roost."

My whole life story—for so many years—was that I was simply incapable of that. Being able to rule my own roost was as distant a dream as a dream of being able to fly. Now I know it doesn't take a lot of complicated psychological work to rule one's own roost. You just start moving the body.

Chapter 19

A Story Comes Undone

"Jump and a net will appear."

—Sally Hogshead

Many years ago I was happy to be teaching classes at Motorola University in Arizona because the company's power and reputation were huge, and it looked as if my work there would go on forever.

Then Motorola got taken down a few notches by some smaller, more creative, more energetic companies swimming around it as though they were piranha. One of those companies was an odd one, indeed. It was called Nokia, and it was not from Japan or Silicon Valley, but from Finland! Finland? High-tech breakthroughs coming from cold and lonely Finland?

Yes, Finland had given birth to Nokia, and Nokia just *tore apart* Motorola with cell phone innovations and breakthroughs that would not stop coming. Social analyst Michael Lewis wrote, "Overnight the Finns had gone from being celebrated mainly for their tendency to drink too much and then kill themselves to being heralded as the geniuses who built the most advanced communications industry on the planet."

Down went Motorola. Down went their "University." It was virtually scrapped as a cost-cutting move in desperate times. Down I went! No more teaching at Motorola. Out I went in search of personal and professional reinvention once again. It hurt at the time, but as is the case with most hurts, it grew into something great once I had regained my perspective. As Lance Armstrong said about his near-death cancer experience and devastating treatment for it: "I owe my life to cancer." (Most people's story about cancer is a little different than that. A recent e-mail from a friend said, "As if turning 60 were not enough bad news, yesterday I found out I had an advanced stage of cancer.")

My friend, author Darby Checketts (whose new book *Leverage* is a very interesting read), recently survived a near-death experience with cancer and went through all the difficult and painful treatments. I sat in his house awhile ago when he told me about being visited by the Angel of Death. He truly experienced the visit!

"The message of the Angel of Death was not that death is imminent or that death is fearsome," he said. "The message was this: *Don't waste your time.* You will die eventually, but death is not that scary. What is scary is to waste your life."

Motorola was a company that had lost such a grip on life. It was sent adrift by misguided loyalty to an old story: the divine right of kings to bestow power. The person in charge of this Motorola—international business colossus—was in charge of it for one reason only: He was the grandson of the founder. He was Sir Chris Galvin, son of Bob Galvin Junior, who was son of Bob Galvin Senior, all presidents of Motorola. Chris had his succession story sewn into his genes.

The boy-king was deep inside his castle, but the peasants were at the gates. It was weird Nokia from Finland that was creating the new breakthroughs in Internet-savvy cell phones, and their very advantage was their *lack* of a story. They were new to this, so they didn't need to hang on to any old traditional ideas.

Then where did they get their direction? Rather than going to the old men, Nokia went to the children. Conceding immediately that young people took to modern technology faster than older, story-bound, curiosity-crippled, and frightened elderly power brokers, Finland studied their young. They kept putting new Nokia technology in the hands of younger and younger people and gathering their product feedback that way.

Meanwhile, back at Motorola, in the most exclusive country clubs around Chicago, men old enough to have watched Ernie Banks play baseball sat and pondered their next moves on a chessboard whose pieces had become covered with cobwebs.

Nokia kept handing research products to their young people and then avidly recording the feedback they got. What they released to the world market took that market by storm. Meanwhile, Motorola kept losing ground.

Michael Lewis, in his mesmerizing book about the future of technology called *Next,* concluded that, especially in the case of Nokia's takedown of Motorola, children enjoy a technological advantage over adults. What is the source of that advantage? *They haven't decided who they are.*

They haven't decided who they are!

"They haven't sunk a lot of psychological capital into a particular self," says Lewis. "When a technology comes along that rewards people who are willing to chuck overboard their old selves for new ones—and it isn't just the Internet that does this; biotechnology offers many promising self-altering possibilities—the people who aren't much invested in their old selves have an edge."

The people most willing to chuck overboard their old selves for new ones are young people. Nokia won because they understood how fresh and unfettered a young mind was. There was no story to drag a young mind down.

And if there *are* older people willing to become unchained in this way, it's often because they are at death's door! Near-death experiences are just that strange and paradoxical. And instructive. Because all your old stories can evaporate in the face of death. And then the worst thing and the best thing start to look to be the same thing. The same opportunity to wake up. Terminal illness is the worst thing, and yet for so many people it was the best thing. Because it gave them a chance to throw their stories overboard. To go to the edge of the boat and drop the story into the sea. How free they became once they did that. How creative. As creative as the children talking to Nokia about what would be "cool" to have on their cell phones.

One day, when Gerard Barber was a clinical epidemiologist and researcher at Memorial Sloan-Kettering Cancer Center, he was examining a terminally ill woman. All of a sudden she grabbed his lab coat. Barber said she "had a grip much, much stronger than I'd thought she could muster—and she instructed me to live my life, 'every delicious second of it.'"

How do we live that way, though, when life is so difficult?

We start by realizing that the internal part of the story of our difficult life is madeup. Because the story of us is madeup. It's just a story. It's just what we say about ourselves. It's what we say in self-defense when someone asks us who we are. But who we *really* are needs no story because it's too alive and awake and at play for that. Too busy living and loving. Too busy laughing and singing. Too busy dancing with life.

Nietzsche said: "Those who were dancing were thought to be insane...."

And when you are at your happiest, that might be what others think of you. Others! Your laughter and your tears may put people off. They may think you are crazy. Just as Nietzsche said: "Those who were dancing were thought to be insane by those who could not hear the music."

Chapter 20

How Does Your Story End?

"This is the end, beautiful friend."

—Jim Morrison

Your story will not set you free. It will simply end. So why not see if you can stop telling it, and let others try to catch up to you. Let others tell your story.

Gandhi didn't have to brag or even tell his own story. He didn't have to go around saying, "Here's what I've done! Look what I've accomplished! I fasted for 60 days, drove the British out of India, and then, for half a season, I pitched for Kansas City!"

Gandhi was simply out there on the road, a human journey, always moving. For people to interview Gandhi, they had to walk alongside him, walking out of breath and talking to him, as he kept his brisk pace, walking across India, setting his people free through nonviolent action, through his own remarkable energy and simplicity.

Anyone can do this. It doesn't take a national crisis to have your life resemble Gandhi's. Anyone can do it.

Anyone. Anytime. Anywhere.

I sometimes work with clients who see themselves as the opposite of Ghandi, the opposite of a successful person—they think they have two or three strikes against them already.

Sometimes I like to recommend the movie *Murderball* to my "unsuccessful" clients. It's a documentary (although a very exciting one) about quadriplegics who play a murderously fast-paced form of wheelchair rugby. It's a violent, exciting sport. But what is so beautiful about the movie is seeing so many young men with at least "two strikes against them" loving life and feeling so much faith and joy. A true inspiration to see. The athletes had to pass through a lot of disempowering stories about themselves: "I'm going to be a cripple, I'm handicapped, I have no life, I'm weird to look at, and this is just too hard." All the stories that started to wrap around them like silk threads, after their accidents. And the movie brings tears and laughter as the men keep trading up. They keep trading their victim stories up to hero-ics: from handicapped person to world-class athlete. From repulsive to attractive. From attractive to happily married family man. And up, up, and up the stories went, stronger and stronger. And in their moments of ultimate joy and action? You could see it. No story at all.

Earlier I quoted the rhetorician Kenneth Burke, who said, "Stories are equipment for living." That they are. They are equipment. But they are not you. Your equipment is not you.

Here's an example of what I mean by that. Much of my work involves teaching people who hate selling to improve their sales. So my challenge is to teach them to love selling and become good at it. It's hard (almost im-possible) to be good at something you hate to do. Why? Because *the story of hating it* is always in the way.

In America, the story about hating selling is deep in our society's psyche. Arthur Miller wrote *Death of a Salesman,* a play about how the profession is so difficult and humiliating that it can kill you. Movies such as *Glengarry Glen Ross* and *Boiler Room,* as fun as they are to watch—and I've seen them many times—further deepen the story that sales is hell on earth. Demeaning and degrading.

Add to that the national historical stories inspired by the Great Depression—stories that cast a spell over us. Stories that convinced us that we could lose everything. During the Depression, men jumped to their death from windows high atop skyscrapers on Wall Street, thinking all the way down, "I've lost everything." But the market adjusted. People went back to work. Everything was corrected. Everything was fine after all. Nothing was really lost.

Many people realized after that that money was just paper. It was not wealth itself, but just a symbol for wealth. Falling in love with money was, as Alan Watts said, "like falling in love with an inch." You are loving a symbol of measurement, but nothing real. Just a story.

But that fearful story got placed in our grandparents' and parents' minds forever. They were caught in the spell. They now thought, "At any given moment we could lose everything. We could lose it all!"

So is it any wonder that everyone in America has some form of money issues? That little worrisome chip has been implanted. We could lose it all.

So to teach people how to get good at selling is a challenge. Because they are asking for money. And what works best to de-program them from its evil spell is to reframe selling as something other than selling. Because the very word *selling* calls up more scary stories than have been written by Stephen King and Dean Koontz combined.

Early in my public speaking career, I loved speaking but hated selling the talks. I was (so my story went) good at speaking and bad at selling. But the catch was, in order to speak, I had to sell. What a bind to be in! What a love-hate relationship with my profession! No wonder I was conflicted all day. No wonder I always felt stuck.

Enter my business consultant Steve Hardison, the greatest salesman in the world. I had seen him perform sales miracles before my very eyes. I also saw that he loved every minute of it, jumping up, clapping his hands, and whooping with joy. (Again the link between loving something and being good at it shows itself.) How could I be more like him? It looked impossible.

"It's not impossible," he said, "but you have to stop selling. You have to learn to sell by *not* selling."

Oh, I see. Hire someone else to sell me.

"No," he said. "You'd miss the lesson. And you can do that later if you want. But for now, you can learn to be great at selling by not selling."

Was this some kind of Zen thing? I wondered. Because if it was, I wasn't into it. Cosmic riddles might be fun for the idle rich to work on, but I had to make a living. I was on the verge of quitting my speaking career and getting a steady job with a regular, dependable paycheck.

"Why would you want to quit something you are so good at?" he asked me.

"Let me see. Because I can't sell it to anyone?"

"Yes you can."

"How?"

"By not selling."

There he goes again. Selling by not selling. It made no real sense.

Then he said, "Don't sell, just speak. Don't go to lunch, speak. Don't get on the phone, speak. Speaking is what you do at your best, so do that. Sell by speaking. It's what you love to do, so do more and more of it. What else do you love to do?"

"I love to write."

"Good! Then write! Don't sell, write!"

He showed me how to do this. And after a few months' practice, I was speaking and writing all day, every day. I was not selling, but I was making big sales! So, as I said, when someone asked me to lunch to discuss using me as a speaker, I would make a counteroffer. I would say, "Are you going to base your decision about having me speak based on how I eat lunch? Why don't we cut to the chase? Why not put a handful of your most trusted people into your conference room, order lunch in, and you eat and I'll speak. Base your decision on that."

People loved it! They signed me up for multiple speeches and seminars. And I loved it, too, because I got to speak. Not sell.

When I did speak somewhere, I invited some sales prospects from other companies into the room to hear the talk. That was the extent of my selling: come hear me talk. I was writing, too! I starting writing my training proposals with as much care and creativity as I wrote my books, songs, and poems, and whatever else I ever loved to write. Love was the key. I would fill my days with doing what I loved.

I wasn't selling anymore, but I was. I know I was. But why try to live inside the limited story known as "selling" when there's always something bigger to live in to? And there's always something bigger.

Now my story was that I was loving my professional life because I was spending my days speaking and writing.

I'd even put a little whiteboard up in my home office. That way, when a difficult "sales call" tried to occur, I would put the person on speakerphone and stand up at my whiteboard and speak! They would ask me questions about my seminars, and I would respond by giving them the best parts of the seminars, my arms flailing, my body sprocketing. I'd even say to the sales prospect, "I am at my whiteboard right now. I am writing three words down. Please write these words down, too." I was in my element. So the sales rolled in.

Soon, as the months went by, I refined this process and trained myself to do this anywhere. I could simply go into my speaker-self at the drop of a hat. Like Jeckyll and Hyde. Boom! I'm the speaker-me, not the shy, sales-hating weakling. It wasn't phony, either. In fact, it was the opposite of phony. "Trying to sell" had me be a complete phony. This was more real. I could do what I loved at any time, night or day. Just turn it on. And clients responded to it because it would give them reassurance that they had the right guy. A truly focused person! They would get a feeling for what they were buying.

In the past, I had sold badly because my would-be clients couldn't connect the dots. They would hear me on the phone. They would hear this hesitant, frightened, self-effacing, obsequious, weak-willed, needy supplicant and *they couldn't imagine* hiring me to speak. How could they? I was gelatin. That's what the story of selling can do to a person. I was weak in the knees. And I am not alone in this. Believe me. I can't tell you how many people who come to me are so good at what they do, but hate "selling" their services. I now tell them, "Don't sell. Just do whatever your service is. Do it for them. They will buy."

Are you a consultant? Start consulting! Already. Give it away? Yes! Are you a painter? Paint them a little something. A carpet cleaner? Clean one of their rooms.

The story of me used to be that I was good at speaking and bad at selling. That was a story that was not serving my life at all. Things are better now because I don't know that story anymore.

"Tell us that story, Dad!"

"I don't know it anymore."

The story of you might also be a story worth *not knowing* anymore. It could be a story worth *not* memorizing. It may be a story worth letting go of—the way Peter Pan let go of gravity in order to fly out the window.

Can I refer, with credibility, to Peter Pan? Was Peter Pan real? Is Santa Claus real? I remem-

ber, as a little boy, being shocked and completely turned around to realize that so many adults
had not told the truth to me about that. What
was their motivation? I wondered about that
for years.

But then I saw that they weren't always truthful
about themselves, either. It wasn't just about
the story of Santa. They would also have a kind
of main story or cover story, or "that's the story
we've agreed to tell" as a family. Self-importance and being somebody is important to
people, and the source of all their misery, too.

Misery and madness, actually. Here's an example of the madness: In the frantic scramble to
"be somebody," especially somebody special
and different from others, we copy others! We
imitate to be different! Isn't that an amusing
puzzle? In junior high school, when it was most
necessary and compellingly *urgent* to get your
story together about who you were, you copied.
I remember so many of the junior high school
boys trying to copy Elvis and James Dean.

I remember in later years going to my own
children's junior high school and seeing that
there were about 100 Britney Spears's walking
the halls, showing their bellies and butterfly
tattoos. A hundred of them. A school full of

youngsters each wearing the button that says "I am unique!"

To find a unique identity, we choose someone else's.

That should give the game away right there.

And it's not hard to find identities to steal. Because we live amidst an embarrassment of entertainment riches. We don't even have to walk down the street anymore without being entertained, earplugs full of the latest music and Chris Rock audio downloads. Drive your car at night and see the ghostly square of a movie being watched in the SUV up ahead by children. Plugged in always. Wasting not a moment. Boredom is forbidden. Silence is forbidden. Be somebody.

But it gets harder to find a unique story to perfect and then stick to. Soon you just end up sounding like the guy you just saw on MTV. Same hand gestures, same clothes, everything the same.

I want to remember that every person is already important, without them having to make up their self-importance for me. Every person. Every moment. I want to remember that there are no unimportant moments. The woman who grabbed the sleeve of the cancer researcher and said, "Live your life, every delicious moment," was saying that to me.

Only our stories get in the way of that feeling. Only our words.

Stories are told with words, and words have chemistry in them. If my story today is that I am just "trying to make a living," my whole brain and body chemistry become low and frustrated. But what if I change the words and instead of trying to make a living I am "creating a life"? New chemistry. Newer, better feelings. Better conversations with people. Excitement. A better life through chemistry.

A flower doesn't have a story about what it is. It just grows and expresses itself. So, when I look at the story of you, I know how hard it's been for you to maintain it. I am very mindful of that. I feel it along with you because I've put such a burden on my heart maintaining my own story!

A young man I will call Joseph recently sat down with me in northern California to talk to me about the heart attack he'd had and how angry he was about the senior managers at his company and all their bad decisions.

After awhile I could see that Joseph had created a comic-book life. His senior managers operated out of another city nearby. And he saw them, occasionally on video conference calls, but they were comic book villains to Joseph and that other city might as well have been an different, evil planet. They were plotting to make him suffer. They were aliens—not human, as he was.

So he had the makings of a great science fiction story going on with inhuman aliens in human form plotting to destroy his mind.

He was the hero of this story. (As all victims are—they are classical mythological heroes—because if they're being *victimized* by someone, well, who's evil and who's good? Read your fairy tales and you'll find out. The victim is the good person.) So being a victim is a misguided attempt at being a hero. Except that it never works. Except that it breaks your heart.

The real hero in life embarks on a journey with a strong heart. The real hero may have been a victim at an earlier stage, but the journey is now everything. The action and excitement in the journey are everything now.

But Joseph and his comic book perception made up a story that literally had attacked his heart. And he was such a good person that I wanted to teach him to relax. I wanted to show him that he had nothing to fear. I wanted to point out to him that his enemies were not enemies. I wanted to show him the humanity—the fears and the tears—in these senior managers so he could relax and realize they were not out to get him at all.

It's not what they are doing that stresses you out, Joseph; it's your *interpretation* of what they are doing. Do you know what an interpretation is? Have you heard of the interpreters at the UN? We are all inter-preters. We all interpret all day. People do things and we are unaffected. Until. Until we interpret, which is to say until we tell a story about it. It's the *story* that hurts.

True success in life lies beyond the story. The amazingly successful Walter Chrysler first said he thought that the real secret of success was enthusiasm. Then he thought about that and changed his mind. More than enthusiasm, he said, the secret is *excite-ment.*

Something wonderful happens to people when they are excited about what they are doing. Excited about that new person they are dating. Excited about that new project they are working on at work. Excited about how the new diet is working. You just know that if they *stay* excited, those activities are going to be successful.

Why is that? Why can't we be burned-out, bored, fatigued and successful? That would make life easier to do, wouldn't it? Maybe so, but the universe doesn't run that way. The universe runs on energy.

So the real determining factor here is how much energy do I create? How much access do I have to my own excitement? How much control do I have over it? Most people think they have no control at all.

Remember the plastic steering wheel you had as a kid? When I was a little boy my parents bought a plastic toy steering wheel that they put on my side of the car so I could think I was driving.

"Oh, look, Steve is *driving!*" they would say with bright and playful voices.

But I knew I wasn't driving. Even though I was only 3, I knew I wasn't controlling the car with my plastic toy steering wheel. You don't have to be an overly gifted child to figure that out.

But we live our lives today with plastic steering wheels, not thinking we're controlling anything, least of all our excitement. We think someone else controls our excitement. (My father, sitting next to me, was really steering the car.)

We think world events, our company, our partner, our luck, our circumstances, and many other outside factors control our excitement. And because we think that, we have a hard time responding to Walter Chrysler's statement that the real secret of success is excitement.

Years ago when I first read Chrysler's quote I thought, "He's probably right. I wish I was excited about something, then I could be successful at it." I hadn't figured it out yet. I hadn't realized that I could bring the excitement *to* the event. I didn't have to wait for some event that was exciting. Excitement is caused by my own created thoughts, not by anything in any event. My thoughts control my excitement. That's actually pretty exciting.

That makes me excited about changing my life from storytime to showtime. I want to go along with Shakespeare. He said all of life's a stage and we get to play a part. Therefore, it's *flattering* to be born into this life: somebody coming up to you and saying, "Hey, we're putting on a play this year and we were kind of hoping you'd star in it."

I'd love to.

Think of the Alan Watts quotation earlier in this book: "The world is a spell, an enchantement, an amazement, an arabesque of such stunning rhythm and a plot so intriguing that we are drawn by its web into a state of involvement where we forget that it is a game."

How do we understand Alan Watts's assertion that it's all a great game? I mean, what about terrorism? Is that a game? Hardly.

But still, life keeps proving Watts right. One way I know he's right is by working it backward. Whenever I, or the people I'm working with, introduce what I call "the game element" into an activity, the productivity and results get better! When we introduce scorekeeping, rewards, prizes, and playful competitions, the results get better and better. Always. Get a game going and you'll increase the energy and improve the results.

So Watts didn't mean to approach life in a frivolous or disrespectful way. Actually it was the opposite. He meant that games are *more* respectful of the moment than a real serious life is. Look at a golfer studying the green before he putts, and look at him as he hovers over his ball in perfect motionless suspension—what focus and what joy when the ball rattles that rattle in the cup! Why can't life itself be that way?

It can.

Only *the story of you* gets in the way. Because the story of you tries to preserve your self-importance. And that self-importance always has you being hurt by others. Always.

Let me give you an example. I was working with a tech project engineer in a computer company in North Carolina where I was consulting. And he and I were trying to talk about job metrics and throughput (subjects I actually love, don't ask me why), and he kept introducing his wife into the conversation. Where did she come from? She came from the pain in his overall, serious story. He wanted to illustrate the hurts he experiences day to day by her comments to him. He's got his self-important story and she doesn't believe it. That hurts. She really knows how to hurt him. His story is that he's a good father. She makes a sarcastic comment that suggests he's not. He feels his story slipping away, so his emotions of hurt and anger rise up. Over and over. Month after month. Year after year.

"Why not just lose this ridiculous story of 'good you and bad wife' altogether?" I suggested, trying to get him back to metrics and throughput. "Let it go."

But he couldn't let the story go. Goodness, we keep repeating our childhoods! Even after I return my tech engineer to the subject of his company, he is now telling me he is sensitive (overly) to how people treat him in the company! Therefore, if someone doesn't return his phone calls, he is hurt. Just as his feelings are hurt if his wife doesn't understand his desire to go fishing with the people in his parish. He is hurt and sad. He talks about things that are "depressing."

I depress him all the more when I say, "A tongue depressor is depressing when it depresses your tongue, but what else is really depressing?"

You know, I hate to take his story away. I really mean that. Because there's some weird, cold comfort for him there. The story of him has his wife in it hurting his feelings at every turn. And his story doesn't stop there, because there were company people who disrespected him, too. Or so he thought. Dishonored him and humiliated him. In his opinion. But is that what they were really doing? Not if you talk to them. Which I did. They were puzzled, almost startled, by his deep hurt and specific complaints. Mystified, to some degree. Their story was different. "We've gone the extra mile for him," they told me.

You sometimes hate to take a victim's story away because it's how the victim maintains self-importance. "Look how *right* I am in this story and look how wrong my wife is." The victim is the hero of the story. Stories are equipment for living! Now the problem with this story is that it is a sad, boring story. Overall. I mean, yes, you are the hero of the story, my friend, but who even wants to listen to this story? That's the real problem with being a victim: The only people willing to listen to your story (for long, anyway) are other victims. So that's who begins to appear in your life, and that's not a good life. Not much opportunity in that life. Victims bring each other down. They don't lift each other up. You want people in your life who lift you up. And the best way to get them there is for you to learn to lift *other* people up. To be uplifting. That's why my cancer survivor friend Darby wrote his book *Leverage* to give readers a way to be uplifting. Darby is fascinated with Archimedes, who said, "Give me a lever large enough and I will lift the world!" I hope my engineer will read a book such as Darby's.

Would that do it, though? The mere reading of a book? Sometimes the answer is yes. Because certain books can really change your life. They have changed mine. And the reason I even ask that question is because of something Franz Kafka said. He said, "A book is an axe to break the ice in your heart."

And I say that the "ice" is your story. The story of you. Frozen over. The winter of your discontent. Look at my engineer.

I now wanted to take his story away, melt it on the spot so he was standing in a pool of water, encased in ice no more.

So I started slowly. I asked him whether it was true, *really true,* for sure, that the people in the company were disrespecting him. Because, I told him, I have talked to them and they think the world of you. And they really did! They thought the world of him!

I said, "Could it be that your perception is not completely clear and accurate? Is that even a possibility?"

He said nothing.

I asked him if it was possible that his wife was scared. And that, when she says hurtful things, that's all she knows to do. That's all the training she's ever had growing up on what to do with being scared. Hurt somebody, disempower the other person so they get scared, too. If you're both scared, it's not so scary.

Chip. Chip away at the ice that we know is the story of him.

The story of you is icy, too, isn't it? Mine is. Don't you feel a chill when you stay in it for too long? Doesn't it chill you to think that you could lose everything and that everything could go wrong and things might not turn out?

When you're really living your life (remember the woman who said, "Live your life, every delicious moment"?), when you're really living every delicious moment, you are not thinking in terms of whether it will "turn out." Because you are living in the present moment. In fact, the phrase *turn out* is a phrase that applies to stories only. Stories *turn out* one way or another, happy ending or sad.

But life? It is to be lived right now. No, not in *that* now. Not in that "now" you're thinking of—the one out there in the "secure" future.

This "now."

Chapter 21

Now We'll Attempt the Impossible

"Attempt the impossible in order to improve your work."

—Bette Davis

My work is often to find a magic key for people to use to take themselves from good to great, and I think I've found it. The magic key to greatness is doing something counterintuitive and pursuing the "hard part" of your work.

Most people don't want to do that. They want to focus on the easy (and soft) part of their work. But it helps more to focus on the hard part. To find what's hard and do more of it. Not less.

Most of us avoid what's hard. Unless we are truly committed to being great. Then it changes. Then we *seek* what's hard.

For example, in sports, in basketball, let's say you want to be great and you can shoot well and pass well, but your ball-handling (specifical-ly your dribbling) is not so good. It's the *hard part* of basketball for you, bouncing the ball across the floor without it being taken away. So now you know that, if you want to be great, you'll do more and more dribbling every day. You'll go crazy with it, as Pete Maravich did as a boy. (Someday you should rent the wonderful bio movie *Pistol* and see how he dribbled the ball day and night, between classes at school, up and down stairs, all the way to the grocery store, from the kitchen to the bedroom. Then he went to sleep with the ball tucked under his arm.) He turned the hard part into the easy part. The best part.

Bill Gates always said that customer complaints (for most company owners—the hard part) were his favorite part of business. He would honor them and study them and build Microsoft's new systems around the secrets they revealed.

Bill Gates became very successful by going to the hard part. He has more than 40 billion dol-lars, personally, and that's a lot. In my opinion. Most of us could get by on half of that. (I al-most wrote that Bill Gates "is worth" 40 billion dollars. Of course, he's worth more than that, and so are you. In fact, the next time some banker asks me what my "net worth" is, I must remember to tell him, "It's infinite." But if he asks me what my self-important story is worth, I'll put some dollar figure on that. I hope I always remember the difference.)

Tiger Woods and his swing coach study videos of Tiger's game, hoping to catch a weakness. Craving a weakness. Yearning for it. Because *that's* what he wants to bring his activity to.

Most of us do the opposite. We want to know our strengths so we can relax in them. Hide out in them. That's why it's really true that what you're good at is exactly what is keeping you from being great.

Many wonderful teachers have written about the subject of mastery, and my own favorite is George Leonard (and his great little book called *Mastery*). In studying people who aren't afraid to go to the hard part, I've worked up my own version of how to master something. How to get great at doing something.

First, consider this question: If you have two sons and one enjoys working with tools and one does not, which one will be better at working with tools? Or: Two daughters. One enjoys playing the piano, really enjoys sitting down to play! The other hates it. Who will, in later life, be better at playing the piano? You know the answers to these questions.

The path to mastery is through enjoyment.

But how do you learn to enjoy something you hate to do?

First of all, decide whether you really want to take it on. You can't master everything. You have to choose. Given the nature of your journey, what skills do you want to master? Then pick one: Do you really want to take this on? Given what you're up to, would it serve you to master this?

If the answer is *yes*, then get going! Time to go through the stages of mastery.

Stage One is fear. I am afraid. I'm scared to try it. Let's say I want to fly my own private plane to places. First, I'm afraid. Remember that learning anything new is potential damage to our self-esteem. It scares us. Some would rather be ruined than change. This represents real change. So, Stage One is fear.

Stage Two is hate. I hate this! I have a flying lesson and I hate these lessons. (Hating doing something is Step Two on the path to mastery!)

Stage Three is neutral. I'm okay with this. I can take it or leave it.

Stage Four is starting to like it. I'm starting to like this!

Stage Five is love. I love doing this. When I am doing this, I am absolutely unaware of the passage of time.

Five stages, each one feeling much better than the one before it. So how do I progress through these stages? The answer is this: by doing the hard part. The more I do something, the more I like it. It's also true that the more I like something, the more I do it—they're both true, but it doesn't matter which you put first. One will always lead to the other. Doing leads to liking, and liking leads to doing (which leads to liking, which leads to more doing.)

You can see how these stages of mastery can be interrupted and sabotaged by stories. If I'm in Stage One, and I'm feeling fear, I might just tell the story that says I'm too scared to even try this practice. If I'm in Stage Two, and I just hate this process, I can just make that my story: I hate this. I can then exit the steps to mastery at Stage Two, with a good story to tell about it. "I'd fly, but I hate the lessons. I hate the studying you have to do." And don't forget the story people have at Stage Three. Do you like working out with weights? "I can take it or leave it. But it bores me."

To truly master something, it's important to know what stage you're in and not freeze yourself at that stage by spinning a story around it. Mastery is best achieved with pure, continuous effort that bypasses and ignores all the stories trying to pull the process down.

This is stunning to me, to realize that the story of me, this story I've put so much time and effort into getting people (and myself) to believe, is actually pulling me down and keeping me from fully enjoying my life. The more I see this, the more I believe that I'm living in a tale told by an idiot.

When Alan Watts talks about the "spell" this world casts upon us, he means we are spell-bound by the power of other people, other nations, and money to make us feel so much fear and anxiety. Watts talks about our story's plot ("a plot so intriguing that we are drawn by its web into a state of involvement where we forget that it is a game")!

When Memphis basketball player Darrius Washington missed his free-throw shots that lost the team the game, he not only forgot that his life was a game, but he even temporarily forgot that his basketball game was a game.

That's how bought-in we get to the dramas we create.

That reminds me of a dinner I had with someone I will call "Leonard." Dinner with Leonard was pleasant enough the other night until Leonard told me he had not had good luck in his marriages, all four of which had ended dramatically. He said he'd not been fortunate. The women were not women of high integrity, and most of them were after his money and had shielded their psychological problems with flirtation. Their stories were better than their reality, Leonard told me.

But Leonard was unwilling to see the part he, himself, was playing in those stories. Relationships are co-creations. They don't just happen to people. I told Leonard that he reminded me of the countless women who have told me about the "jerks" they got stuck with in marriage. As if they had nothing to do with co-creating the relationship that led to marriage.

They just got hit out of the blue by a jerk. As if somebody in the upper universe had a "jerk gun" and just shot these women with this gun in multiple drive-by jerk shootings, and then these women all got together later and shared stories about the jerks that they got hit with and married. What gives that story so much life is that other women support it, and soon it diminishes the chances of ever finding a good relationship because it all seems so random.

We scare ourselves unnecessarily with our stories about jerks and bad wives. We spin the tales that create our own fear and dysfunction. This is a phenomenon that my friend Ron Hulnick has built an entire university to solve. Ron and his wife, Mary, head up the University of Santa Monica, and their deep personal vision is to help alleviate all the unnecessary psychological suffering in the world that they believe is caused by people failing to see that they are divine beings. People think they are "mere" human beings locked and lost in psychological struggle with other humans. They just don't understand their divine connection to spirit. People's internal stories about themselves are almost always negative because they've been programmed that way.

The communications people first heard about themselves were largely negative because those communications were being made to teach and correct. "Your room is a mess. How could you be failing math? Where is your homework? Please put on something else before we go to Grandma's. Stop teasing your sister. Why don't you ever listen? Will you please try to show your classmates more respect?"

Does this bring back memories to you? When the subject was you, the story was usually negative. Oh, you got nice things said to you here and there, but they were never said with the same passion and certainty as the critical negative things. So you never really believed the good things about yourself. You never trusted them.

And unless your upbringing had a strongly playful spiritual component, there wasn't much for you to do but create a permanent story around your defects and disappointments. (You'll never, *ever* forget the day your father said he was so very "disappointed" in you.)

Those were your guardians. But you can't blame them. They were trying to get you ready for the world. As though bundling you up tight for the snowstorm. Little human beings trying to survive the storm.

"But we are not human beings trying to have a divine experience," says Ron Hulnick, echoing Chardin. "We are divine beings having a human experience."

Now you can see right through the story of you.

And as with that DVD you just rented, your story can have alternate endings. Or how about—even better—no endings at all. In fact, maybe there's not even a story. Just you, just me, just now. In this present moment.

When you are right here, right now, you are a tiger. Ready to spring.

William Blake wrote his powerful poem about the "Tiger, Tiger burning bright, in the forests of the night"—and the fire in that tiger's eyes, the fire that consumes life's problems, the fire of the spirit that burns bright when the mind and body are in action.

Which is why the cure for any block is to spring into action. Writers who are "blocked" and can't write are blocked into a *story* about themselves. To cure the writer's block (and many writers go to many lengths to try to cure this profession-killing psychological horror), writers simply need to abandon the story that says, "I can't write these days. I sit down to write and nothing comes forward." The cure is to write anyway. Write nonsense. Write a bad chapter. Just write and write and write. It's amazing what happens for writers when they do that. The writer's "block" is broken. The words are now flowing freely from spirit to the mind, then from the mind to the brain, then from the brain to the hands, then from the hands to the keyboard, and from the keyboard to the forests of the night. And the cycle is spinning again as the world whirls and the heavens dance and the writer becomes a poet.

***

Billy wanted to thank me. He shook my hand and said that he attended a seminar I gave a couple months ago about leaving your victim story behind and owning your life. Owning your spirit. Owning your story-less excitement about the next actions.

Billy said he had a brain tumor and was sitting in that seminar with a "valid" victim story about having a brain tumor.

"I would say that was valid," I said.

But Billy said that what the seminar woke him up to was his ability to own things he wasn't owning. Including his choices about how to respond to his pain.

"I just accepted the pain as part of my victim story about having this tumor," he said. "What you got me to see with the victim thing was that I might have choices. I hadn't really tried everything. I almost *enjoyed* telling people I was in pain all the time."

Billy dropped that story and took action. He confronted his doctor with how ineffective his pain medication was. He insisted on getting something that worked. His doctor jumped on the problem, and soon had Billy on a completely different pain management program. It worked just fine and Billy now felt great every day. He even pulled his new pill bottle out of his pants pocket and held it up to show me.

"I'm pain-free," he smiled. "At least for today. But that's enough for me! Who has more than today?"

I was pleasantly surprised by Billy's new story because I had been all too quick to grant him a justified victim story the minute he said the words *brain tumor.* We tend to be intimidated by those kinds of things. But at that moment, he was more of an owner than I was. It was one thing to *teach* the concept of ownership, quite another to do it. I felt as if I was coach Charlie Lau watching the student George Brett hit .400.

George Brett learned from coach Charlie Lau about hitting because he was willing to go through the stages needed to master it. Brett was exceptional. Many of today's athletes are not. They often appear prematurely in the obituaries, dying of gunshot wounds or drug overloads. Or they are arrested for murder, or involved in gambling scandals. And soon you start to realize that all that money and all that star power wasn't enough for them.

When you, yourself, are not enough, nothing else is enough.

Money doesn't convert to happiness. In fact, it can be the very thing that makes happiness feel unreachable. Because it can take away the incentive to make a big effort. It can make it feel unnecessary to take a heroic journey. The hero's journey is then replaced by trying to buy pleasure to cover the void.

Recently, NBA basketball guard Jason Terry was asked by a magazine writer how many TVs he had, and he said, "Over 50."

I read that answer and I wondered, wouldn't 40 televisions be enough?

How much total entertainment can you get from those 50 TVs? Would you have them all on at once? What fun!

Apparently Jason Terry just kept adding TVs. Because one option, if the story of you isn't making you happy, is to keep trying to *add* to the story. Add travel. Try to collect experiences and accumulate postcard moments all over the world. (Would travel have the same value for you if you weren't allowed to tell people about it? You can go anywhere you want but you can't say where you've been.) Or adding objects—some people add art objects to their story; some people buy companies to add to their story. Some buy cars and then make sure other people see them in those cars.

Bill Gates is going in the other direction. He's all about philanthropy now. He's giving his money away. He added a lot to his story, but now he's giving it away, the way a plane dumps fuel before a crash landing.

As we saw, resume enhancement is another way people add, absurdly, to their story. Also, new wives and lovers can put your story back on the covers of magazines. (I don't care what you're saying about me, just spell my name right. I know it's now possible to have no talent, accomplish nothing at all, and just be famous for being famous.)

Returning to the moment takes us out of this madness. Returning to the timeless moment. This moment is eternal, which doesn't mean endless—it means *beyond* time. Where we go when "time flies." Where that linear clock—ticking off the passage of time—is no longer in operation. (Stories need linear time to exist. They need a beginning, a crisis, and an end.)

But the joy of smacking one out of the park needs no such thing. Boom! The ball is just gone.

So the trick is to lay the story of you down. Set it down on the ground, and then proceed. Setting this story down is like setting down a backpack full of rocks and running free for a little while. Maybe you'll even want pick up a tambourine. Now you're dancing, one hand waving free, silhouetted by the sea. We go to music to get on another vibratory wavelength. And we dance. The beauty of the dance is that you are not dancing to get anywhere. You're not going to be dancing from point A to point B on the floor. That's why it's funny when people say "I'm dancing as fast as I can."

People can dance, chant, sing, or repeat a prayer or mantra over and over and it becomes mesmerizing—the way "Hey Jude" ends, over and over, on and on, into infinity.

When we enter that moment of re-circulating eternal time, we so often do so while doing something we've put a huge amount of effort into. A distance runner's ultimate high. The "zone" athletes get into. Timeless moments on stage for a musician. The height of their success is determined by the depth of their struggle. Writers also report finding these timeless moments, quite often, on the other side of an all-out war with writing badly. Writing badly, writing badly—ZOOM!—into another world of pure flow.

Many times, writers, painters, and artists say, "I don't know where that work came from! It wasn't me! It came *through* me." All inspired work is that way—even the inspired work of a good parent—finding just the right thing to say at bedtime to take a child's fear away. Finding just the right combination of leftovers to make a marvelous family dinner with "I don't know where I got that idea. I thought I was tired when I entered the kitchen and all of a sudden I just found myself getting into it." Divine beings having a human experience.

And it is this practice of setting the backpack full of rocks down and getting into it that makes it all worthwhile. That's the real joy right there. Taking a mere task and converting it into something you're really into. You learn to dance with it. Or to take a sad song.

And make it better.

T.E. Lawrence knew the false nature of stories about good and bad fortune. About sad songs of our own composing. The story his men tried to float to him was that it was God's will that the camel boy was lost to die in the sandstorm. Lawrence rode back and saved the boy to write his own fresh story.

And so it can be with the story of you. If you woke up this morning, you have a fresh page to begin writing on.

And the sun that came up shines for you.

"As a man's real power grows
and his knowledge widens,
ever the way he can follow grows narrower:
until at last he chooses nothing,
but does only and wholly
what he must do."

—Ursula K. Le Guin
A Wizard of Earthsea

Recommended Reading

Brown, Michael. *The Presence Process.* New York: Beaufort Books, 2005.

Checketts, Darby. *Leverage.* Franklin Lakes, New Jersey: Career Press, 2006.

Dauten, Dale. *The Max Strategy.* New York: William Morrow & Company, 1996.

Goss, Tracy. *The Last Word on Power.* New York: Currency, 1995.

Kurzweil, Ray, and Terry Holland. *Fantastic Voyage.* New York: Rodale Books, 2004.

Leonard, George. *Mastery.* New York: Plume Books, 1992.

Lewis, Michael. *Coach.* New York: W.W. Norton & Company, 2005.

_____. *Next.* New York: W.W. Norton & Company, 2002.

Nabokov, Vladimir. *Strong Opinions.* New York: Vintage, 1990.

Weil, Andrew. *Healthy Aging.* New York: Knopf, 2005.

Wilber, Ken. *The Simple Feeling of Being.* Boston: Shambhala, 2004

_____. *One Taste.* Boston: Shambhala, 2000.

Wilson, Colin. *The Essential Colin Wilson.* Berkeley: Celestial Arts, 1986.

Wolfe, Tom. *Hooking Up.* New York: Picador, 2001.

About the Author

Steve Chandler is one of America's most beloved public speakers and authors. His books have been translated into more than 11 languages throughout Europe, China, Japan, and Latin America.

Chandler spends most of his time as a public speaker. He was once called by Fred Knipe, a four-time Emmy Award–winning PBS screenwriter, "an insane combination of Anthony Robbins and Jerry Seinfeld."

He was recently featured in an episode of NBC's *Starting Over,* the Emmy Award–winning reality show about life-coaching. Chandler temporarily joined the faculty at the University of Santa Monica to teach in the graduate program of Soul-Centered Leadership.

Chandler has been a coach and leadership trainer to more than 20 Fortune 500 companies worldwide. He graduated from the University of Arizona with a degree in Creative Writing and Political Science, and spent four years in the U.S. Army in Language and Psychological Warfare. He was once a journalist, but never won any awards of any significance.

Chandler is the author of numerous books, including *RelationShift* (with Michael Bassoff; Robert D. Reed Publishers, 2003); *100 Ways to Motivate Yourself* (Career Press, 2001); *Reinventing Yourself* (Career Press, 2005); *50 Ways to Create Great Relationships* (Career Press, 2000); *The Joy of Selling* (Robert D. Reed Publishers, 2003); *17 Lies That Are Holding You Back* (Renaissance Books, 2001); *Ten Commitments to Your Success* (Robert D. Reed Publishers, 2005); *100 Ways to Motivate Others* (with Scott Richardson; Career Press, 2004); *Two Guys Read Moby-Dick* (with Terrence N. Hill; Robert D. Reed Publishers, 2006); *9 Lies That Are Holding Your Business Back* (with Sam Beckford; Career Press, 2005); and *The Small Business Millionaire* (with Sam Beckford; Robert D. Reed Publishers, 2006).

He may be reached at his Website: www.steve chandler.com.

If you have a small business and have read Steve Chandler and Sam Beckford's *9 Lies That Are Holding Your Business Back and the Truth That Will Set It Free,* you can further your exploration into successful business by visiting the Chandler and Beckford business Website at www.smallbusinesstruth.com and learning small business lies Number 10 and 11.

Books For ALL Kinds of Readers

At ReadHowYouWant we understand that one size does not fit all types of readers. Our innovative, patent pending technology allows us to design new formats to make reading easier and more enjoyable for you. This helps improve your speed of reading and your comprehension. Our EasyRead printed books have been optimized to improve word recognition, ease eye tracking by adjusting word and line spacing as well as minimizing hyphenation. Our EasyRead SuperLarge editions have been developed to make reading easier and more accessible for vision-impaired readers. We offer Braille and DAISY formats of our books and all popular E-Book formats.

We are continually introducing new formats based upon research and reader preferences. Visit our web-site to see all of our formats and learn how you can Personalize our books for yourself or as gifts. Sign up to Become A (RHYW) Registered Reader.

www.readhowyouwant.com